I0211969

The Truth Well Told

The Truth Well Told

And some lessons in humility

PAUL CONQUEST

First published 2016

Copyright © Paul Conquest 2016

All rights reserved. No part of this publication may be
reproduced, stored in a retrieval system or transmitted
in any form by any means, electronic, mechanical,
photocopying, recording or otherwise, without the prior
written permission of the publisher and copyright holder.
Paul Conquest asserts the moral right to be identified as the
author of this work.

Typesetting by BookPOD

Printed and bound in Australia by BookPOD

A Cataloguing-in-Publication entry is available from the
National Library of Australia

ISBN: 978-0-9954121-0-1

INTRODUCTION

It was the blood. Waking up in the morning with everything red. My hands were thick with the stuff and it was caked under my fingernails. Looking at my shirt, drenched in claret, my first thought was that I'd murdered someone.

My guts twisted. I went cold. Still deep in an alcoholic fog, my memory of the previous night was a blank. I was home in bed with my girlfriend, and that's all I knew for sure. 'Sharon... Sharon,' I whispered, staring at the horrible mess. 'What the fuck have I done?'

~

When I was twenty-eight, my regular drinking haunt was the Bracken Ridge Tavern. I basically lived there, from Friday lunchtimes till Monday mornings when I went back to work. If it wasn't at the tavern, it was somewhere else I could drink. Non-stop drinking and smoking every weekend. Always. That was my life. I was making loads of money, spending it just as fast, and my life was going nowhere.

That night I'd been blind drunk, as usual. The Bracken Ridge Tavern was packed and all my friends were there. Apparently, I'd been talking to one of the crowd, Jeff Farrier, when someone nudged me from behind making me spill beer over Jeff's shirt.

'Sorry, buddy,' I said. 'I didn't mean to spill my beer over you.'

'That's alright, mate,' he replied, promptly pouring his beer all over my front. 'I didn't mean to spill my beer over you.'

It might have been a joke but, obviously, I didn't find it funny because I flogged into him. I didn't stop punching the absolute shit out of him until a bouncer came up from behind, put me in a choke hold, and I fell unconscious. Eventually, I began to remember the terrible, uncontrollable murderous rage I'd gone into when Jeff drenched me with beer. That horrible rage must have been there waiting for a moment like that to come flying out. At the time, I had no idea why that happened. I thought it was just my lifestyle coming back to bite my arse. But it definitely wasn't the end of that particular nightmare. In fact, it was only just beginning.

I woke up outside the tavern with my front teeth loose. They'd been pushed in. I was told later that the bouncers had dumped me outside and then, because of the awful towelling I'd given Jeff, allowed Jeff to kick the crap out of me.

Hearing all of this made me feel really bad. I was wracked with remorse. I didn't care at all about the beating Jeff had given me. I just wanted to make it right with him and, because of the massive amount of blood, find out if he was OK.

That phone conversation didn't go at all well. He gave me a huge spray about the pounding I'd given him, and then told me to go and fuck myself. There was only one thing left to do — head off to the tavern, of course.

I was sitting on a bar stool in the middle of a game of pool with my brother when it happened. At first, it was a feeling of intense anxiety, followed by light-headedness. My heart was racing and felt like it was going to burst out of my chest. I was frightened. Very frightened. I started to have flashbacks. I had no control over my body. All I could hear was background voices but couldn't understand what anyone was saying. Background conversations and the feeling of pins and needles all over, dizziness and a drugged feeling. Nausea came quickly after that and I couldn't catch my breath. I wasn't drunk; I'd only had a couple of beers. I even thought that someone had spiked my drink.

The flashbacks reminded me of when I was fourteen and my big brother lived downstairs in our family home. Both my older brothers used to take a lot of drugs back then. They were spaced out most of the time. They would take heaps of drugs of varied kinds but their main drug, day in and day out, was marijuana. They never worked; they would just sit around smoking pot all day.

At that age I was very impressionable, wanting to try some of those drugs. I threatened to tell our mother if my brother didn't let me have a go. He gave me a cone of pot that absolutely knocked my socks off. He told me that it was laced with horse tranquiliser, and I thought I was dying. My head felt like it was exploding and I had a massive panic attack. I had previously experimented with a little marijuana, but I had never had anything like that before. It lasted for about two hours and I ended up going to sleep. The next morning, I was alright again.

~

At this point in my story my life sounds terrible, doesn't it? And me a pretty horrible sort of guy. I'd have to agree, and there are times in my life that I'm not particularly proud of.

However, over time, there's plenty I believe I've done right in my life.

I didn't know it at the time, but that night in the Bracken Ridge Tavern was just the beginning of a changing man. A self-made man. It was the start of a bumpy, often scary journey that I'm still very much on today. So let me take you back a bit further and we'll start filling in the gaps before you decide to toss me on the dump.

GIDDY HEIGHTS

When I was around three-years-old, we went to the Royal Brisbane Show, commonly known as the Ekka. It was brilliant because my grandfather used to be a police inspector back then, so we had a letter allowing us to go on any ride we wanted.

Mum was afraid of heights, although I wouldn't have been aware of that at the time. Going from ride to ride, we ended up on the Ferris wheel. Because of my age, Mum had to come with us and she began to become hysterical as the wheel started going up.

My brothers, one eight-and-a-half and the other ten, being a bit wild, rocked the carriage backwards and forwards so that it swung madly. Mum started screaming and crying and I was really traumatised seeing her like that. We went higher and she got even more hysterical. The carriage stopped right at the top so people at the bottom would be allowed off. My brothers kept rocking and swinging the thing and Mum went nuts. Making things worse, I started yelling, begging her to stop my brothers.

This incident made an enormous impact on me, and it wasn't until much, much later when I had therapy for my fear of heights that it became clear from where that fear originated.

Seeing my mother exhibit extreme terror that night, handed her fears to me on a plate. Even now, just thinking about the rocking, swinging carriage makes me want to wet myself.

It was one of the most terrifying moments in my life. I'd always climbed trees and walls like any other kid, so I'm convinced I wouldn't have reacted if my brothers hadn't played up and Mum hadn't demonstrated such great fear.

Ever since, heights have been a problem for me. Not average heights. I'm good up to four or five stories but, after that, I freeze up and have a panic attack. I've been going to counselling and hypnotherapy to overcome it.

I first started the hypnotherapy in 2001 because I wanted to go to a convention in Cairns. It was three months out and I thought, *I'm definitely going to do this, I'm going to get on a plane and fly there.* So I booked my flight, started the hypnotherapy, and it was all planned to happen.

In the last week, I was so nervous and on the toilet non-stop. On the morning of the flight, I'd almost lost it, but managed to turn up at the airport with my bags. Breathing deeply, I checked my stuff in and went to hop on the plane. The flight was delayed by two hours. That did it. Sitting there watching the planes taking off and landing, I lost my nerve, got up, collected my car, and drove the twenty hours to Cairns. I just made the convention and have still never flown. That was the closest I got.

Another close call involved Jordan Belfort. In 2015 we had an important joint venture meeting in Melbourne with Symonds Homes. Jordan organised a private jet to get down there. I was humming and hawing while Jordan organised some girls to distract me on the flight. The day before, I pulled out and drove to Melbourne, had a two-hour meeting there, and then drove back while Jordan flew back on the jet. Bit of a nuisance really.

The hypnotherapy has taken the edge off it a little, but what's taken the edge off it even more was Jordan organising some neuro-linguistic programming (NLP) for me last year. It has had good results. I've not finished and not followed through on it because a lot of other stuff has happened since then, as you may have heard, but it's been good. Now I can go to the twentieth floor of a building and it doesn't worry me too much.

Strangely, it hasn't really impacted on business here in Queensland but it has impacted on the growth of business around the country. For that very reason I like to think this is the year that I'm going to move past it because I want to expand into Victoria.

Yes, yes, I know you want to know more about my association with Jordan, the supposedly demonic, criminal wolf who turned out to be anything but— later OK.

FIRST SIGNS OF ENTREPRENEURIALISM

When I was a young fellow, I never really saw much of Mum and Dad. My Dad was a concreter and, after work, would be out drinking with his mates. Mum worked night shift behind the bar at a pub and, for one reason or another, wouldn't get home until 2am.

My brothers would look after me, and I looked after myself a lot. You have to remember that this back when kids were left on their own a lot. Around our way, a housing commission area in Bracken Ridge, it was completely normal. Everyone walked to school too. In grade one, I walked twenty minutes there alone — something unheard of now because there's a fear of kids being snatched or run over. Back then, the area was one big community; everyone knew everyone, and people watched out for each other.

One day in grade one, I wagged school and spent the day in a concrete pipe. Yeah, I know, I know. Walking to school, I'd always go through the back of some shops and this particular day I found huge pipes there. I climbed into one and stayed there until I saw everybody coming out of school. I have no idea why I wagged school that day. I obviously just didn't want to go, and maybe it was somehow the beginning of my interest in the construction industry.

Mum and Dad fought a lot, so we moved to my grandfather's place at Bribie Island for a fresh start. Mum and Dad reckoned they'd try to keep the marriage together until we were old enough and then they'd split up. Until they actually did that when I was seventeen, they still fought continuously.

Dad was very unapproachable when we were young but that changed when I turned fifteen and went to work for him. Before that, I really didn't know him at all. I think that was pretty standard with families back then. Dad was to be feared but he was never physical with us and never hurt us. We'd just make ourselves disappear as soon as he got home.

At the time, I never thought of him as an alcoholic, but he drank every day without fail. So did Mum. They'd have a lot of friends over on the weekends. They played cards and always had a barbecue with lots of social drinking going on. They drank during the week too. After work every day Dad would have at least six tallies (four-and-half litres). Mum would have after-work drinks at the pub and then come rolling home pissed.

It still surprises me now that we thought that to be the norm. Mind you, it wasn't until I was twenty-eight that I came to see things differently. I learned then that there was more to life than the one I'd learnt from my parents.

As a kid, I always wanted to be someone and I always wanted to make money. At nine I had two jobs, one selling *The Telegraph* on the nature strip in the middle of Beams Road at 6am. Then at 3:30pm I'd go to a chook farm and collect eggs for two hours. An old Italian couple owned it — lovely people.

I didn't work because there was a shortage of money at home. As much as Mum and Dad would drink, smoke and argue, there was always food on the table, and whatever else we needed. We wouldn't necessarily keep up with the Jones's with our clothes and shoes, but we'd always have our bikes and skateboards — the things kids our age considered important.

For me, working was more my ambition to want to get ahead and to have good things in life. At nine, it was exciting for me that I could afford to get my hair cut at the barbers instead of having mum cut it, something she'd done all our lives. It was exciting that I could go and buy McDonalds myself. Saving up for many things, I fondly remember buying new wheels for my bike.

Up at the news agency that I used to sell the papers from, I'd buy raffle tickets. You could buy them off the shelf so a friend, Ricky, and I would go around selling raffle tickets on the weekend, making out that we were selling them as a school raffle. We'd pick up around twenty dollars for a Saturday morning's work — a lot back then. Pretty bloody bad when I think back on it.

Ricky and I would steal Mum's passion fruit from the vines that ran down the back yard and the chokos she was growing. We'd sell them door-to-door and make a killing. Mum laughs about it now, but she was really mad at us at the time.

My brothers were that much older than me and, as much as I love them, they've always been hopeless. They had a different biological father to me too. They were about three and four when dad came along. We're completely different. They got into a lot of drugs and got into a lot of no-good stuff. I didn't fall into the drugs scene at all, maybe because I saw a lot of the mistakes they made along the way which steered me away from it. Around fourteen or fifteen I smoked a little bit of pot, didn't enjoy it, and never took it any further than that.

From an early age and despite occasional problems with staff, I think I was keen to build an empire. However, I lost my paper run when I was ten and it really upset me. We were going on holiday to St George where we went twice a year to fish. I had no choice, I was told I had to go so I let the news agency know that my brother was going to be taking over my job for the week I was away. My brother Michael, known as Ducky, told me he'd do it. When I got back and went to the news agency to make sure everything had gone well while I was away, they told me that as I'd gone off on holiday and no one had turned up to work, they'd given my job to someone else.

I still remember the tears welling up as I stood there. I have trouble thinking about it even now and how horrible it was at the time. I loved that job more than anything, Ducky knew it and just never turned up for it. Ducky thought it was funny, laughing about it to this day. About six months later I got my newspaper run back when my replacement lost his job.

Back then I used to dream of owning a house, then it was how many houses I'd need to get a certain amount of rent to be able to buy another house each year. I was already doing the maths in my mind, far before it was actually feasible. I imagined I would be someone one day and wasn't going to let anything stand in the way. I'd go out riding around the streets with my friends — a normal thing to do back then — but I'd be looking out for work.

When I was twelve, we stopped and spoke to a house builder. He was constructing a home with really rough looking bricks on the outside. I got a job working with him every Saturday and Sunday for two months smoothing off the bricks with a hammer and chisel. I was always looking for something to do to make money, and thinking about what I would build with that money in the future.

Ricky had been my best buddy from grade five right up to when I was seventeen. We did absolutely everything together. We'd continuously come up with crazy money making schemes. Apart from the passion fruit and choko business, we'd buy dice at the local news agency, take them home and drill holes in them, and then glue valve caps into the holes. We'd sell them to everyone at school and it became a craze with kids screwing them onto the valve caps on their bikes.

If our parents went away for the weekend, we'd organise a party, buy some booze, and have a cover charge to get in. We'd make plenty of money out of that. There were failed ventures too. Once, when Mum and Dad went away overnight, we had a party at my place and the house got trashed. The toilet door got kicked in, there were holes in the walls, mum's rocking chair got destroyed, and I got into a lot of trouble. I would have been thirteen at the time.

Ricky and I had a bit of a falling out and a punch-up when we were seventeen. I haven't really seen him much since then. Now he's in prison for drug trafficking, so he took a different road to me.

~

When I was about nine, I wagged school for two weeks straight. It started with me being scared because I couldn't do the assignment that was due that day. I knew I'd be in trouble. On my way to school I went to the toilet in the public loos near a caravan park and decided to stay there, all day, in that cubicle. It seemed like a good idea and, crazy as it seems, I much preferred spending my day there than going to school.

The second day I did exactly the same thing. I went there and stayed there, listening to people come and go until I thought it was time to walk home. Coming up my street, I ran into a boy, Robert Farr, two years older than me, sitting in his yard. He called me over.

'What are you doing,' he asked.

'What do you mean,' I replied. 'I'm on my way back from school.'

'But it's only 2pm,' he said.

That was lucky. If I'd gone home then, my parents would have known what I was up to. Instead, I hung around with Robert for an hour and chatted before heading home.

Robert then had a chat to his brother, Jason, who was the same age as me. Jason decided to join me wagging school, so the three of us went fishing in the woods the next day.

Over the next couple of weeks we did all sorts of things hanging out together. It couldn't last. Two weeks later I came home and found that Mum had received a letter from school asking if I was alright. I'd been caught out and, that night, the police came around. I was shocked and terrified, little knowing that my parents had arranged the visit, thinking that getting the cops to give me talking to would give me a fright. And it did. Very much so. Of course, everyone at school found out about my adventures fishing in the woods and for the rest of my primary school days I was labelled 'The Fisherman'.. Not that I actually caught any fish.

Unsurprisingly, I was bored at school, and I've always put that down to being kept back at kindergarten. They thought that I wasn't mature enough, so I ended up always a year older than my peers. I didn't struggle with the school work or anything, I was just bored. Because of that I didn't buy into anything that was going on and would rather have been off doing something else.

I was an incredibly shy person and still am deep down. People sometimes find that hard to believe, but I'm a little bit awkward in crowded situations, or where there are lots of bubbly, outgoing people. That's when I don't talk much.

When I was thirteen, a girl called Colleen had a crush on me. She had a friend, so Ricky arranged a double date with them. Out the back of our school at Boondall was bushland and a paddock full of wood chips designated as our meeting place. The idea was to do some kissing and canoodling. Never having done any of that before, I was too terrified and didn't turn up.

About two weeks later, Colleen's friend cornered me down in the toilets of the Boondall Entertainment Centre and made me kiss her. This was the first girl I'd ever kissed and I was petrified, I had to get out of there as quick as I could. I didn't enjoy the experience at all, but then she went around and told all my friends that I didn't like girls. Back then the word used was 'frigid'. 'Paul's frigid!' they'd yell. 'He doesn't like girls.' Because of that shyness, girls really unnerved me and I didn't date until I was fifteen after I left school.

By the time I was almost fifteen I'd been wagging school and fishing a lot since that first time. My parents spoke to my school who told them that school was good for some people, but it wasn't necessarily good for everybody, and an apprenticeship could be a better option. Mum and Dad agreed that if I found a job when I turned fifteen, I could leave school. Of course, I had one organised well before and started it on my fifteenth birthday.

Work was a whole different world for me. I'd skip school in a heartbeat, but not work. I just loved going to work and I loved making money. I'd tried to get an apprenticeship; mum had driven me around all the construction sites but there was nothing. So, ironically, I ended up finding a job at a factory that made school furniture. It was three suburbs away and I would have to catch the train there at five in the morning and come home about five at night. I was only there for about six months but I absolutely loved it. My job was laminating table tops, so I was spraying glue and cutting laminate. If I did two hours overtime every day and a further four on Saturday, I'd take home one hundred and seventy-eight dollars which to me was massive money. All my friends were still at school and I was the man with all the cash. We used to drink a lot. Back then, a hundred and seventy-eight dollars could buy you a lot of bottles of rum or Passion Pop!

In the beginning, I had big plans for my money. I saved around $3000 and was putting the majority of my pay away every week. That's when I started going off the rails. The heavy drinking started. I was hanging out a lot with my friends, and always in the city chasing after girls. I never got into drugs or anything, but I got a girlfriend and she was expensive. Within four weeks all my savings had gone — three thousand hard-earned dollars and nothing to show for it. For a year I had to lie to my parents about it because they were really proud of me for saving all that money. While I kept my stupidity a secret, they'd tell people how well I was doing. It was a new and horrible feeling knowing I'd had so much money and was back to having nothing. I could have done so much with it — bought a good car, for example. Unfortunately, I hadn't learnt my lesson and my stupidity wasn't about to stop.

I went through a period in my life where drinking and having fun really took over. This isn't a cop out, but I think back to the environment we were brought up in and I know it influenced the way I behaved. As much as I loved money, wanting to get out there and do anything to make it, growing up with parents who squandered every penny they ever had made it seem alright. We were always eating take away, they were drinking and smoking and going to the races, and that was just the normal thing to do. I wasn't doing anything different to what everyone else was doing. It's a throw away kind of lifestyle.

The wasteful period of my life lasted until I was twenty-eight, when I stopped drinking and smoking on the same day. I drank a massive amount up until that night at the Bracken Ridge Tavern. Apart from my encounter with Jeff, I wouldn't say I was a horrible drunk, but I believe I was an alcoholic. Strangely, I wouldn't drink during the week because of work. But on weekends I was a lunatic. Right from the age of fifteen it was all about getting drunk. I can't remember a Friday or Saturday night that I wouldn't be off my face at a pub, or a club, or a casino, or at the races until I turned twenty-eight.

IT'S ALL ABOUT WORK

After my six months at the factory, I got a job with a lawn mowing company. I was there for another six months and I loved that job too. It was energetic and busy, but it wasn't really going anywhere.

At sixteen, I went to work for my dad in construction and that's when I really got to know my old man. I learned what life was really about. We'd travel to work together and work closely on the job. He used to sub-contract to other companies and I'd be working directly for him. At that stage it was only the two of us. Most of the time we built things like sound barriers for fencing companies. They would be around schools, along railways, and factories.

By the time I was twenty-one we started employing people. Before then, I'd leave Dad around every six months, work somewhere else and, when I came back, I'd be on more money. At sixteen, when I was on $40 a day, we had a big argument. He was a hard man to work for. If it was nearly forty degrees and I got caught going for my water bottle twice in the same hour, I was in trouble and got a clip around the ear. We never had lunch breaks because he felt they were a bad habit and took too long. When Mum had a go about it, he'd say, 'Fuck off, you're teaching him bad habits.'

We'd do a lot of digging holes without a bobcat — all manually. If there was hard ground, we used a crowbar and shovel. We didn't have a concrete mixer back then, so we'd mix it all by hand. A bit later, we were allowed to hire a mixer if the job required more than a cubic metre of concrete. Under that, I had to do it in a wheelbarrow. I was always praying that if the job required a mixer there was a hire shop nearby. Even then, if the first shop we went to didn't have a mixer available, Dad wouldn't waste any time looking for another — it was back to the wheelbarrow. He was tough and, at work, I was just another employee. That's the way he was brought up; 'if it was good enough for me, it's good enough for them' was his philosophy.

A few times I left Dad and walked home fuming. *Fuck this*, I would think. *There's more to life than this*. But, the next morning, there I was back in the ute. When I really got jack of it I'd find another job somewhere else for a few weeks. Then Dad would ask me to come back, and I always did — for more money. By the time I was twenty-one I was making $300 a day so there were a lot of pay rises in between. That's when he made me his business partner and, from then, I could easily take home $4000 a week. It was fantastic money back then, especially with my rent being only $150 a week. I like to think that I was a good worker and we did make a very good team.

I got on better with Dad once we'd become partners. I think he considered me a man by then and had more respect for me. He respected my opinions and the arguments weren't there anymore. We seemed to gel and we both agreed on a lot more. It makes me think of the old saying, 'Hire a teenager while he still knows everything.' I was probably a young know-it-all in the early days so I couldn't blame him for being angry at me. As the years have gone on, he's softened more and more.

Dad continued to work up until about five years ago and, he was still digging postholes by hand, still doing all the same hard work, and funny to watch because you could have twenty young guys on site, all twenty to thirty years old, and the sixty-year-old man is going to show them up as he always did. He still hasn't lost that part of his anger. If he sees someone not working as hard as they should, he'll walk up, push them out of the way and shout, 'Gimme that fuckin' thing! Let a sixty-year-old man show ya how it's fuckin' done!' That's his attitude. It really makes me laugh. These days he's still in good health and travelling around Australia in a caravan.

When I was seventeen we were renting in Boondall. Mum always wanted her own home and, although she and Dad had been in separate bedrooms for twelve months, they put a deposit down on a house in Burpengary and decided to try again. Dad was working on the new Myer Centre, earning insane money drilling anchors into the rock. I was off concreting somewhere and he was bringing home $3,000 per week, so in six months he had enough for the deposit.

The old man and I changed our entire lives for her. I didn't have a car, so I'd always be on the train from the middle of nowhere to Brisbane to see my friends, and Dad and I had to get up in the middle of the night to start work early in the mornings. It lasted three months. Mum got a job at the Bribie Bowls Club, met a guy there, fell in love, and left us high and dry. She later married him and they stayed together for twenty years. I still struggle with remembering how one night I was asleep on the couch and woke up to hear my old man sobbing on the phone with her, begging her to come home. She'd called him to break up with him because of the guy she'd met.

One of the worst things is to see a parent crying and in so much pain. A part of me expected her to come home eventually, and Dad would have had her back in a second. He would talk seriously about killing himself, didn't sleep much for twelve months, and became a wreck for a good year. It took a while but Dad eventually got over it and re-married.

A few months after Mum and Dad broke up, he and I moved to a flat in Northgate. That's when I started drinking a lot more. I began going out with Dad to the races and was going rapidly downhill. The trouble was that I stayed there for a long time.

I was always doing something at night and saw little of Dad in the evenings, so he wanted to move in with Steve, a mate of his, who's become a good friend of the family. I moved into a place with my brother Duane. Steve was great for Dad. They had an absolute ball together, so the next few years were really good for him. He hadn't dated in twenty-five years so Steve showed him the ropes, got him into the dating scene, and they'd be double-dating and getting up to all sorts of shenanigans that we can't mention here.

The downside of that was my moving to Racecourse Road in Hamilton. There I was, either at the races at one end of the road, or the Hamo pub (Hamilton Hotel) at the other. If I wasn't at work, I could be found at one of those two places. I'd really broadened my horizons, hadn't I?

I had good days and bad days at the races. My Dad, his Dad, all my uncles, they all loved the races. They loved gambling and they loved horses, so it was pretty well bred into the whole family. I think the more you go there the better you get at it, and you get better at reading the betting forms and the race guide. You might have good days but you can't win 'em all.

From the age of twelve, Dad used to take me to the trots. We'd go either to the Redcliffe trots on Friday night or the Albion Park trots on Saturday night while mum was working at the pub. Many times going home on the bus with Dad, I was absolutely terrified of what Mum was going to say when she found out we'd lost all the money. We'd blow the whole bundle and we'd be on our way home with nothing, and no rent or money for food. We were living on the edge of nowhere.

From fifteen to seventeen I had a girlfriend, Melanie. I absolutely loved her. She used to live at Coorparoo and I was at Boondall. She'd come over on Friday afternoons and stay the weekend. On the Sunday afternoon I'd drop her home and wouldn't get back home until midnight on Sunday night. We did that for two years and I was crazy about her. She was my first girlfriend, a year older than me, and I didn't know anything else at the time. It ended sadly.

When she turned eighteen, Melanie started going out to the pubs and clubs with her sister in the city. I chose not to go to those sorts of places. I used to go to local pubs near home, the ones I'd known since I was fifteen. The very first time I ever went to the Hamo, which, unbeknown to me at the time, was to become my haunt for two years, was when she told me she was going there with her sister. It used to be called Cinderella Rockefeller back then and there were two hours of fifty cent drinks downstairs, and three hours of them upstairs. Maybe it was the other way around, but there were five hours of cheap drinks.

That night, I snuck in there to see what she was up to. Her sister hadn't shown up and Melanie was with a group of five guys. I watched her head off with them, leaving me feeling upset so I drank quite a lot. I actually had a good time and made new friends. The following day, I questioned her about it and she broke up with me. It turns out she was already seeing this guy, Bucko, one of the guys she left with, and it broke my heart. She married Bucko and the poor man died of cancer two years ago.

After that night at the Hamo, I spent every Friday and Saturday night there for the next two years. It probably started me off on a new a tangent because I met lots of girls in the place.

About four years later I was at the Hamo when I saw Melanie and she came up to talk to me. She was nice, gave me her phone number, and said, 'If you're ever looking for a good time give me a call.' I wasn't seeing anyone at the time, so obviously said to her, 'I'm always looking for a good time,' and went home with her that night. The following morning she woke me up at around ten o'clock to rush me out the door saying she had to get up because her boyfriend was off on a ride with his motorcycle club and he was due back at lunchtime. I had to get out of there. He was a bikie! That was the last time I saw her.

Drink driving has featured considerably in my life. I'm really ashamed of it now because I went through a terrible phase where I was had up for drink driving five times in a twelve-month period. I was disqualified from driving for five years and, at twenty-one, went to jail for a month. That certainly hammered home the difference between right and wrong for me and I didn't drive again until my disqualification ended.

One of the biggest things I experienced in jail wasn't being scared of the people in there, as you'd expect. It was the feeling of losing all rights. I simply didn't have the right to make any decisions for myself; people told me when I would eat, drink, get out of bed, go to the toilet, and be allowed outside. It's someone taking away all my liberty — that was tough. I was reduced from being a person to merely being a number which is demeaning. It's a feeling which made me never want to repeat the experience. I'd learnt my lesson, but I was feeling a bit sorry for myself so I dramatically increased my drinking.

Part of the reason I kept working with my Dad for the next five years was because he'd pick me up for work every morning and drop me off every afternoon. I was between a rock and a hard place. When I lost my licence, it was for a minimum of five years. You actually lose your licence for life, but you can reapply for it after five years.

It's not granted automatically. I started applying again after five and a half years. I had to get the documents, do a couple of courses, get letters of support, do an alcohol psychology course, and reappear in court to show the magistrate that I'd changed.

I was on the edge of twenty-eight and beginning to realise that life was passing me by in a blur. Every Friday for three years — go to the pub at lunchtime with Dad, drink steadily until six, meet up with my mates and drink with them until ten, and then head off to a nightclub until 5am. Then off to the casino until the pubs opened at ten to do it all again. I'd be really sick Monday through to Wednesday, then have a few beers on Thursday to be ready for a full-on weekend again. There's no doubt about it, I should have been dead. And after that night in the Bracken Ridge Tavern, I often wished I was.

OUT OF THE FRYING PAN AND...

One of the most powerful things that changed my whole life was anxiety. I suffered with depression and anxiety all my life but didn't know. It's a very hard thing to talk about because it's regarded as a weakness. We don't understand it, it doesn't make sense to us, so we don't talk about it. There you are! You've heard it from me.

I saw Jeff, the guy I beat the shit out of, about five years later at a 711. He was ignoring me, so I walked over to his car and said, 'Hey buddy, a lot of water has gone under the bridge and I just wanted to say I was sorry... still sorry about that night. Is there anything I can do?' 'Go fuck yourself!' he said. 'Don't talk to me! I don't want you anywhere near me. And you can pay me the five thousand it cost to fix my teeth.' I had noticed that he had really nice looking teeth. Maybe I'd done him a favour. Regardless, I'd done my best to make amends for something I'd been feeling terrible about for all those years. Now I put it behind me.

Back to that Sunday after the fight. Remember, I was having what would be the first of many bad turns. Unless anyone has ever experienced it, they will never understand how awful it feels. It happens to one in ten people but they seldom talk about it. I didn't know what was going on in my mind and I thought my body was shutting down. That was terrifying.

I immediately left the pub, caught a cab home to my place, and stuck my fingers down my throat. I made myself throw up because I thought that someone had spiked my drink. I just couldn't shake the feeling. Then I couldn't sleep that night because the fear and anxiety prevented me from calming down.

The feeling went on all day, and couldn't get to sleep until about nine o'clock that night. It was the worst day of my life, but what I didn't realise was that it was just the first day of the worst *part* of my life.

At that point, I had no idea that it wasn't going to go away. Every day for the next two years I had those feelings at the same level, and then, over the next two years, the symptoms eased a little. I am still controlled by anxiety and there are things I don't do because of it. It has never completely gone away.

I woke up on the Monday morning and was stunned to find I still felt anxious, nauseous, light-headed, had pins and needles all over, and suffering the same palpitations. Panic set in. I didn't know how I was going to get through the day.

I never told anyone, not even Sharon, for about two years. For those years I kept going to the doctor to have blood tests because I was feeling lethargic. I was hoping the blood tests would show I had glandular fever or a definite condition that was making me sick. I was constantly looking for things that were wrong with me.

All the tests were coming back clear, showing that I was healthy. I knew that I *wasn't* healthy but I didn't know what was making me feel the way I was. None of it made any sense. It was something I couldn't talk about and I didn't tell the doctor.

I just couldn't understand why I was getting these feelings of fear all the time, the pins and needles and feeling faint.

I even considered that it might be the hormones in KFC because, one day after eating it, I started to get those feelings really severely. I didn't eat KFC after that and, if I did, I would get a panic attack. But I was also getting the attacks when I wasn't eating the chicken. Then I had a drink of Coke and had another panic attack. I thought, *well, maybe it's the Coke*. So then I gave up Coke.

What I found out many years later was that these incidents are called associated anxieties. The Coke, the chicken and also chocolate weren't giving me anxiety, but because I was thinking that they might, my brain associated the things together in my unconscious mind and I would have an anxiety attack if I consumed any of them.

That Sunday, the day of the flashback, was the day I stopped drinking. I never, ever drank again. Sharon, who was later to become my wife, also stopped drinking that day. I told my shocked friends and family that I was done drinking and I wanted to change my life around, which was true. I just didn't give them the details. I just couldn't handle what was going on and I think I'd truly hit rock bottom.

I look back now and if God made that happen to me I thank Him for doing it, because He did me a favour. If I'd continued down the path I was on, I would be long dead.

For the next few years, I became a bit of a loner. Once I stopped drinking, smoking and going out to nightclubs, supposedly having fun, I didn't have the same friends. I had nothing in common with them. Also, because of the anxiety, I had a social awkwardness. I would avoid situations where people could make me feel worse. If I bumped into those people from back then now I wouldn't even know what they looked like. There was a bit of a cut-off point. Those people who I saw from day-to-day back then, I never saw again.

About a couple of years after the first anxiety attack I realised it was an emotional or mental breakdown. I started to read books about what was going on with me and I began to get an understanding of what was happening. I went back to the doctor to get the anxiety seen to. All the doctors wanted to do was put me onto drugs, Zoloft or something else.

I believe there is a reason you hit rock bottom and it generally has to do with your lifestyle or your mental health. I didn't think that drugs were the way to go — I thought that medication was a Band-Aid. The doctors told me I would never get better without taking the drugs. I said, 'Fuck them!' and I'm now about ninety-five percent.

I have little things happen but I know how to control the anxiety, and I understand what is happening. What works for me is not to take the drugs but to understand what is going on with my body, and then I can then deal with it.

But, at the start, I had no understanding whatsoever about what was going on. I couldn't fathom it. If I couldn't explain it to myself, how could I explain it to anyone else? There was simply nothing to talk about. It was the worst time of my life, and I didn't know why. I wish I had talked about the anxiety at the time. That's why a lot of people kill themselves — because they don't talk about it, they'd rather take matters into their own hands.

I've had thoughts of being a social worker off the back of all this and helping others in the same situation, because it was the worst thing that had ever happened to me. I now have a greater understanding about how one feels. It is hard to understand unless it has actually happened to you.

What also became obvious to me was that it was very hard for people to understand. At the time, every day, I couldn't wait for sleep at night. I was being put out of my misery and I was annoyed every morning that I was going to have to go through the same thing again. It was such a shitty time waking up and such a happy time going to sleep.

To this day I have a television in every room of my house. The reason is that watching television is the only way I can get my brain to stop working. When I am awake I am thinking about this or that and I can't stop. When I find a movie I really like, if I watch it over and over I can still enjoy it, but I can switch off to it. The stimulus to my brain fades off and I can get to sleep. Now it is the only way I can get to sleep.

I would love getting home from work and putting my TV on. I never ever stopped working or trying to moving forward with my life. I still got up and out of bed of a morning even though I could have switched the TV on and watched that and let my brain switch off, but I couldn't bring myself to do that. I remember reading a book at the time and it said if you have all these symptoms, congratulations you have earned yourself three months off work or you won't get better. I couldn't do it. I couldn't take time off work and I couldn't do it to my Dad because we worked together as partners. I was too busy, even then, trying to get ahead. I was still pushing forward and, who knows, it may have taken an extra ten years to get better.

Every year, I've measured myself against the year before and I would see a little improvement. I'd be drinking Coke again because I'd overcome that. The following year I'd be eating chocolate again. These days I can eat a whole bar of chocolate.

I still get the feelings every now and then. I still get the numbness and the symptoms of a panic attack coming on, especially when I am stressed. At the time, I had an eye twitch that lasted for three years. People didn't notice it but I could feel it. To this day the eye twitching is a little tell-tale sign that things are getting too much. When I get that twitch I generally back off for a week or two. I just let myself catch up. I guess that's my fuel gauge these days.

I pushed on consistently over many years. You learn a lot about yourself and how to control the anxiety. You can turn any negative into a positive. That was the biggest negative of my whole life — I was at rock bottom and at my worst. To be reminded so strongly that I was at my worst helped me to become my best.

I also wondered at that point what would force people to kill themselves? Why would they commit suicide? I could never understand how life could get that bad. I always believed that there is a light at the end of the tunnel and things are eventually going to get better. The lesson I took from what happened to me was that things are never as bad as you think they are going to be. It actually goes both ways. No matter how good or bad things are going to be they never are. Ever.

It is hard to see why someone would end their own life. Before the anxiety I couldn't understand that and neither could Dad. I had an argument with him one day. Something came up about suicide on the radio. He was saying how weak those people were that do something like that.

I had never spoken about the way I had felt, but I was feeling that way day in and day out. All I wanted to do was go to sleep at night and not wake up. My days were absolutely shitty. And that's how many people feel and it's why some people kill themselves.

Before the anxiety I never thought I would feel that way and, now, it is hard for me to imagine how I felt back then. It doesn't make any sense to me. When I was sitting in the car with my dad and he was talking about how ridiculous it was that people do that to themselves, and how could they possibly do that to themselves, I argued with him. I felt so strongly about it at that time, that I would have jumped off a bridge at the snap of fingers.

Even though I couldn't see daylight or a way out, I wouldn't have done that to my family because I love them and it would be horrible for them. Sometimes that's the only thing that keeps you going. The easy way out for yourself is to just not to have to go through this day after day. I so understand why Robin Williams, the comedian, killed himself. A lot of people probably don't understand because they have never had to struggle with that condition. It's not about being sad because you don't feel anything at all. You are emotionless.

I have an enormous sense of humour and in those early years I did retain my humour. I still enjoyed movies like *Pulp Fiction* and *Bad Boys*, they were my favourite movies at the time. I would repeat the one-liners even back then. The joy for me is the ability to make others laugh.

I often take the piss out of myself, not others, to make people laugh. That's about the natural ability to build rapport. I still retained that ability to build rapport throughout that stage of my life because I was still trying to get ahead. A big part of that is making them laugh a little bit — making them feel like you are good friends and building their trust. I am a very animated person, making jokes and speaking with my hands. I wouldn't do that if I didn't mean what I was saying. I put myself out there being myself.

Building a business is about relationships. With me it is all about building a culture and building up people. The first thing

I do when I turn up to work is say 'hello' to everybody, shake their hands and have a laugh with them.

I make sure I do that every day. It doesn't matter whether you are the janitor or the CEO, I will try to make you feel important. I know that's what is going to build the culture and that is what is going to build the team. It's everyone coming together. The biggest lesson of my life is the art of treating everybody equally no matter who you are or what you do. If you do that you are going to get respect back from them. A sense of humour is a big part of that.

~

For that ten years after the Jeff incident, I was working on myself and getting better and better, but I was still not there. The doctors wanted to put me on drugs because they thought there was a chemical missing in my brain. Well, I believe that ninety percent of the time there is a reason our brain is not producing it. My body was not there yet and my body was not ready. I didn't want to put a Band-Aid over it and be comatose for the rest of my life.

I went to Glenn Chandler to have hypnotherapy for my fear of heights. It was the best consultancy I've ever had. We started to talk about my fear of heights, which is another form of anxiety, and then about my panic attacks and how I had been having trouble with anxiety my whole life. He explained to me how the human body works.

When the fight or flight mechanism is activated, the body pumps all the adrenalin into the parts of your body that need it. Into the arms if you are going to fight or the legs if you are going to run. That happens automatically, the unconscious part of the brain does that.

The problem with that happening is, if you have an imbalance between your unconscious thinking and your conscious thinking, your unconscious is telling you it is time to be scared, so you get the pins and needles and your heart is racing. That is anxiety and anxiety is the feeling of fear.

Your unconscious thinking tells you when to feel fear, which is a healthy thing. If you are on top of a skyscraper and go to the edge of the building, no matter how comfortable with heights you are, you're scared of jumping off that skyscraper. That is your unconscious thinking making you scared for the right reasons, because it wants you to live.

If you have an imbalance it's telling you to be scared at the wrong time. It's an associated anxiety — like the time I had anxieties around the KFC or the Coke. Your unconscious thinking tells your conscious thinking to be scared when it shouldn't. It makes so much sense when it is explained correctly and the condition is so much easier to overcome and far less frightening when you understand what is happening with your body.

When I first met with Clem Chandler and he revealed what hadn't been explained to me he said, 'Nothing annoys me more in life than doctors that prescribe all those drugs for a condition that they won't fix'. They were his exact words.

Doctors won't listen to someone like a hypnotherapist because they don't believe in that sort of thing — they don't see that as healing or proper medicine. They'd rather prescribe the drugs. If they actually talked to someone with the condition and worked out how their mind works, the drugs are simply not necessary. They just mask the condition.

The doctor keeps putting my wife Teena on Zoloft because she is depressed. I say, 'Fuck the Zoloft, let's just change our lifestyle and our way of thinking. You don't need the drugs'.

Marriage, and Children – the Ones I Knew About

Even through all my dark, dysfunctional days, I've always worked hard. I was never unemployed for long. If I lost my job one day, I'd have another the next. I can't stand the thought of being unemployed or not doing anything. I can't see the point of not moving forwards. If I'm feeling under the weather and take a day off sick from work, by that afternoon I find myself lying around feeling guilty, aware that I haven't done anything or achieved anything that day.

It's hard for me to stand still. I seldom take holidays and when I'm forced to I get stressed out thinking what I could be doing, what I should be doing, and what I'll be doing when I'm back. I'm due for a holiday now and I need it because of the family.

My uncle George was a workaholic, he'd go to work at five in the morning and get home at nine o'clock at night. He was a tree lopper and everyone ridiculed him saying he worked too hard, he was only going to kill himself, he was working himself into a grave, and so on. I now think that's a limiting belief, because as you get older you realise that someone like that goes to work because he enjoys it, not because he has to go to work. That's what he wants to do with his life. Myself, I like getting up in the morning and going to work. If I'm enjoying what I'm doing I don't see it as work. It's only work if you're not having fun.

After I stopped drinking, the first couple of years were a blur. In the first month I was glad to go to bed at night and go to sleep. I wasn't so happy to wake up in the morning and get going again. I would rather have just slept for a month. Other than that, I can't remember too much about it. But I do remember longing for stability. I wanted to get back into society and do normal things. So for those first few months I'd wake up at four in the morning and go buy a paper to find out where garage sales and flea markets were happening. Then I'd buy old cupboards, sand them back, and restore them. I'd go out and haggle on Saturday mornings at someone's garage sale just for something to do, then take the purchase home and work on it. I did that to occupy myself, and the other thing I did was become attached to the girl I was seeing at the time, Sharon. We'd been together for about six months and I married her a year later. I really settled down and I guess I was trying to find myself.

Before I gave up drinking Sharon had put up with a lot. Besides being a boozy larrikin-type, I used to sleep with a lot of other women, and I think she was vaguely aware of it. She was a great woman and still is. I have two children with her.

I met her when I was sharing a house with Dan, who became a very good friend. We met because he was advertising for someone to share his house in Deagon and I answered the ad. He'd just broken up with his girlfriend so I moved in. It wasn't until twelve months later that he mentioned to me that he'd actually advertised for a female to share accommodation and he was quite taken aback when I answered the ad. It turns out no one else answered it. Anyway, he ended up being my best man at both my weddings.

He was a young carpenter and was on the straight and narrow, he never drank or smoked, and he was very clean living. When I moved in, I showed him a whole different life. I probably ruined him too. I took him under my wing a little bit and we became best buddies. We used to go out and always get a lot of girls.

Dan's mum used to cook us meals and put them in the freezer for us. She really looked after us. One day she turned up with some meals and found the girl that Dan was seeing mowing the lawn, and Sharon inside cleaning the house, while Dan and I were on the veranda drinking beer. She gave us quite a spray over that. Twelve months later I moved out with Sharon.

When I gave up the booze, Sharon and I had to find new friends because we had nothing in common with the old ones. It was really tough for the first few years, it was a different lifestyle, but I was never tempted to go back. Before then, if I didn't go out on a Friday or Saturday night I'd feel like I was missing out on something. I don't even know what it was I was looking for, but I was looking for something. And yet nothing would change. Every time I went out, it was more or less the same — a bit like watching *Neighbours*, you can go back to watching it three years later and you haven't missed a thing.

I met Sharon when we were out drinking one night. She was a talker, which was a great match for me because I wasn't much of a chatty type in those days. She can talk underwater. She talks and talks and talks. And I wouldn't have to say anything. I'd go out on a date with Sharon and wouldn't have to make conversation because she'd take care of all that. It was great.

We'd actually been in the same classes in both primary and high school but we'd never really spoken or had anything to do with each other until we met one night in the Hamo. She had a boyfriend at the time, but we hit it off and I started hanging out with her for the next six months, then we started dating.

When we decided to get married we moved into her parents' house, Jim and Diana, so that we could save a deposit for a house. Her parents are fantastic people, she's got a really lovely family and I feel bad saying it but when we decided to split up I was more upset about losing her family than I was about losing her. I would get home in the afternoon and have a shower and by the time I went to bed at nine o'clock at night, my dirty work clothes would be clean, dry and hanging up in my closet. That was not Sharon, that was her mum. I think if I'd had an opportunity to marry Sharon's mum, I certainly would have. If I had to get up at three in the morning for an early start, I'd try to sneak down to the kitchen and get some breakfast. But, as soon as she heard a footstep, she'd be up and insisting that I have a hot breakfast before going to work. She is an incredible lady.

Sharon and I lived there for twelve months before we moved out together and got married. I'd still be with her today if she hadn't become so high maintenance, but I've only got myself to blame for that.

When we first met, I used to be a total arse. I'd be out drinking all the time and bringing different girls home when she wasn't there. She'd catch me out so, rightfully, she didn't trust me a great deal. In fact, not at all.

When we were married, she became very possessive. If I went to the RSL with her dad for a couple of hours, I came back to the third degree. 'Were there any girls there?' 'What were they wearing?' 'Were you looking at them?' And, 'I bet they had short skirts on.' If we were walking through the shopping centre and there was a girl wearing a short skirt walking past, she wouldn't be looking at her, she'd be looking at me to see where my eyes were. She was constantly like that, every day, so that became a big thing for me. She is an absolutely fantastic person and the guy that's got her now is very lucky because they wouldn't have that type of relationship. They haven't got that history and my track record of infidelity.

But we get on really well, she has a nice partner whom I employed for a couple of years so I got to know him, and we're all friends. Also we've got the kids, so it's really important that we all get on well.

There's a bit of a funny story around the arrival of the kids, although it didn't seem very funny at the time. Lachlan came along after Sharon was trying to get pregnant for six months and he was two when I ended up leaving. When we split up, she told me that she didn't care, she just wanted to have kids, and if I didn't give her kids she was just going to go and find someone else to have kids with.

After I left Sharon, I started sleeping with my receptionist Teena, who is now my wife. She was about twenty-one and I was maybe thirty. We were on and off, and we argued, so things were a little bit rocky between us.

I'd been sleeping with Teena for about six months when we had a big argument. She moved back up to Bundaberg to her parent's place for a few weeks, so we weren't seeing each other. We were on a break, essentially. During this time, I went over and visited Sharon. I'd visit regularly to see Lachie, and I'd often stay the night. So, this time, I'd gone over there and had gone to sleep on the couch when Sharon woke me up. I ended up sleeping with her.

Two months later, Teena and I had patched things up and were back together when she gets really excited. Yes, she's pregnant. *Whoa*, I'm thinking. *This was just having fun. I don't want a baby with her. I'm not ready for this.* Well, big mouth here told her just that. And she lost it. Really lost it. She was punching and kicking walls and doors — the works. I have to tell you that I'm ashamed about how I reacted back then. Looking at Joe now, I wonder how I could have thought any of that, let alone say it out loud.

Now you're wondering about that night with Sharon, aren't you? Yes, Sharon calls me up three weeks later to tell me she's pregnant too. Now I've got these two women pregnant, they both want the child, they're both so excited about it, and I didn't tell them about each other. Did I come clean with Teena? What do you think?

Two years later I got a letter in the mail from the child support agency just updating me on some details. Teena opened it, read it, and rang me. 'Do you have anything to tell me, Paul?' she said. I felt such relief. I had so wanted it to come out, but I didn't know how to do it. I felt like such a coward not telling them. It was probably the worst thing I've done in my life, and is the thing I'm most ashamed of.

I went home and explained to Teena what had happened and how the situation had come about. She was so angry with me, but not about sleeping with Sharon, not about having a child, what disappointed her so much was that I thought so little of her. That I thought she wouldn't understand. She was angry at me for what I'd done and how it was so unfair on Sharon, 'that poor little girl'. Within two days she'd made a room for Emmy, had put her name on the door and told me, 'If you think that little girl's going to go through life without you doing the right thing, you've got another think coming.'

I get a lump in my throat thinking about that, it says so much about my wife and how I underestimated the sort of person she is. I never saw that coming. It was one of the worst things you could do to a person and I feared that if I told her she'd be gone, but it was quite the opposite. She embraced it and Emmy's been part of our family ever since.

At the same time I went and told Sharon about Joe. I came clean. She was angry too but she'd been angry with me for the past two years anyway, so she was no more angry than she had been. Overall I thought she was okay with it, but then I wasn't living with her and didn't have to witness her emotions on a daily basis. She did call me a liar and regularly called me a child molester because I was living with a girl eleven years younger than me. That makes me smile because she's now living with a guy eleven years younger than her. I do mention it from time-to-time and the whole story has become a little joke now.

Two years after Joe's arrival, we had Billy, and we've got another one, Toby, who arrived three years later. Teena would desperately like a girl and although she considers Emmy her daughter, she'd love to have a biological one of her own. So I'm not out of the woods yet.

My kids all get on fantastically well, in fact people often mistake Emmy and Joe for twins. They look so much alike so it's easy to make that mistake. Then there's one more, I have a twenty-one-year-old daughter from when I was twenty. A girl, Cherie, was up from Melbourne and we slept together. When her dad, Bob, came to pick her up, he asked me if I wanted to come down and stay with them for a while. We had hit it off so I went down there for a few months.

When I was back in Brisbane, she called, mentioned that she was pregnant, and that I was the father. I was conveniently sceptical at the time. Apart from that, I was only twenty and didn't want any part of it. I was an absolute arse. I did ask her if she wanted to move to Brisbane because after two months in Melbourne, I knew I didn't want to live there. There was no work the whole time I was down. If there had been work, I would have been keen to go.

I was a bit of an arse after she said no. I didn't contact them, and I didn't have anything to do with them. Then, seventeen years later, I started getting text messages from someone I didn't know. I thought it might have been an ex-girlfriend from years gone by. They were random, 'How are you going?', 'I wouldn't mind getting to know you', 'I haven't seen you'. I had no idea who it was. I'd been working and living in Bowen at the time and I was on my way home one day and I got another message. I'd been sending replies saying; 'You've got the wrong number, please stop messaging me,' that sort of thing. It's a long drive home from Bowen, so I decided to mess around with whoever it was. The message asked, 'Why did you leave me?' I thought, *What? How did they even know I'm driving out of Bowen*? I messaged back asking, 'Who is this?' I got no response so I rang the number. It was a girl's voice. 'Who is this,' I asked. 'Why are you messaging me?' This shy, young voice said, 'What do you mean? I didn't do anything.' 'Well you did,' I told her. 'I'm just returning your call on this number. It was definitely you calling me and I've asked you to stop messaging me.' She said, 'I don't know what you're talking about, I didn't message you.' So I said, 'Alright, whatever, stop messaging me now.' and I hung up.

Then she messaged me and said, 'But what if I wanted to get to know you like I should know you?' And when I say a young girl, I didn't think seventeen, I thought early to mid-twenties, something like that. So I messaged back; 'What are you wearing?' I was thinking, *Stuff it, I've got a long drive home, I might as well see who this is, or get a bit of a rise out of it.* She then sent a nasty message back saying, 'I can't believe you, you've got a wife and children!' *Oh shit,* I thought. *This is someone who knows me. How could this be?* So again I asked her who she was. She then said that if she told me, I probably wouldn't want anything to do with her. I asked her why and she messaged, 'I'm your daughter!'

This was the last person I thought of, and I'd just asked her what she was wearing! I thought, *Fuck! What's wrong with me?* It was a crazy situation, but it sparked something in me. Suddenly, I wanted to know her, so I flew her to Brisbane (because I don't fly).

Natasha came and spent a week with us. We really hit it off and she started coming to Brisbane regularly. I went down to Melbourne for her eighteenth birthday and caught up with her mum and her family. Then, when she was nineteen she came to Brisbane to work for me and she's been working for me ever since. When she first came up she lived with me for twelve months. She's fantastic. She became a really intelligent, lovely young woman.

MATES AT WORK

There's a friend I've known since I was a young fellow. We've worked together and done lots of things together, but he's always been an absolute rogue. I found myself working for *him* at one stage, something I never thought would happen. But this is really about how I got into the contracting game, so let's go back again to when I was twenty-eight.

I'd been working for the old man on and off for many years, always sub-contracting. We started off with Boral Cyclone then moved on to a few other companies along the way, and wherever we were working, this other guy, Paul Cameron, always seemed to working there as a sub-contractor as well.

The difference was that Paul Cameron had to hire absolutely everything; a wheelbarrow, a shovel. He didn't own anything, and every bit of money he'd make, he'd gamble, either at the TAB or I'd give him a call and I'd hear the pokies in the background. He was just hopeless with money. He'd been like that his whole life.

Along the way we ended up both sub-contracting for another company called Fencepac, working for a salesman there called Sylvester. We knew him as Silver and, in my opinion, that guy was, and still is, the best salesman in the fencing industry.

One day, Silver had it all out with the owner of Fencepac and then moved to another company called Aotea which was owned by some Kiwis. Dad and I kept working for Silver because he used to pick up large government jobs around the place, and we'd subcontract to him. Paul stayed with him too.

We'd been with him for a year and, by then, I'd stopped drinking and was working really hard. We'd brought a truck and a bobcat, built up a bit of a team of workers, and we were doing very well. Our intention then was to go out on our own. Dad and I were going to start up a company and planned to ask Silver to work for us as a salesman. It looked really good.

We were getting very close to that when we came into work one day and Silver had great news. He was going into business with Paul Cameron! So Paul had beaten us to the punch. It's funny, I can't remember any time in my life where I've been in a business transaction with Paul Cameron and won. He was always just one step ahead. He's a bit of a rogue and there are so many funny things that have happened to us over the years.

Silver was still the guy that won all the large government contracts in Brisbane at the time, so Dad and I found ourselves working for him. That meant we were working for Paul Cameron and he was paying the wages. Silver told us how Paul had changed his ways. He'd been working really hard, getting big contracts, and saving all his money which he'd been putting aside. He said, 'I can guarantee that you're going to get paid, that you'll be looked after. I'll win the work, you're going to do the work, everything's going to be fine.'

So, it's a month later and we haven't been paid. Silver's had to put some of his own money into the company to keep things afloat and he's found out that Paul didn't have any money at all. It was all bullshit. He hadn't been paying any of his taxes, he hadn't been paying any of his accounts around town, so at every turn he owed money and everyone was in a predicament, including us.

We were now owed six weeks' pay. Silver asked us to stay on board and he'd asked many companies to give him trade accounts. He's got a great name in the industry and it took him years to establish that trust and respect. So, for the next twelve months, it was all about robbing Peter to pay Paul at every turn, just to keep the company afloat, saving Silver's and our names, and try to get things back to where they needed to be. And we did; we stuck it out and stayed for the next twelve months.

During that time, Silver and Paul would fight a lot. Money would come in and Paul would spend it on things like a two-thousand-dollar barbecue or treating himself to the nicest car, or whatever he fancied. We were pretty much stuck. The company was in Paul's name, but it was Silver who had guaranteed everything, and his credibility was on the line. The business would never have got off the ground without Silver's reputation.

Silver won a job for us on the Bruce Highway. This was good for us because it was on the north side and quite close to home. If we got paid we were going to do well out of it. And here comes the turning point for me business-wise. We were working away one day when Silver turned up just to have a chat. It was a strange and unusual thing to have a chat out on site, and he mentioned to Dad and I that he wanted to tender on fourteen kilometres of railway fence out of Warwick and the bids were to close in about three days' time. He explained that he was confident that he could win it but felt uncomfortable winning such a good job for Paul Cameron. 'Such a fantastic job,' he said. 'And you guys would make so much money.'

So there was Silver selling us this fantastic job, saying he didn't really want to quote it because he was sick of getting fucked over by Paul Cameron. 'We need a way out sooner or later,' he said. 'I just don't know what to do.' And off he went.

I went home and started thinking about what he'd actually said, which is precisely what he wanted me to do. I realised that he was baiting us a little. Without actually saying it, he wanted us to go and price it ourselves, or do some deal with him. He was baiting us for a little bit of undercutting.

The next morning I woke up, rang Silver all excited and said, 'Mate, I've got an idea. Why don't I go and price that job? You tell me what I need to do, give me the contacts, and we'll go halves in the profits.' Silver says, 'Wow, there's an idea. I never thought of that! Yeah, let's do that then.'

And that's exactly what happened. It was a big rush the next day. I had to ring the railway inspector up at Warwick and race up there to look at the job as he wouldn't allow us to tender it if we hadn't actually seen it. At the same time, we had to get the accountants on board with registering a company for us overnight

It was a mad rush to estimate the job. For obvious reasons, we knew where we needed to be dollar-wise to win the work and, two days later, the tender closed. They rang us and said that we were the cheapest tender but they didn't know much about us. They then rang Silver and the railway inspector said, 'You guys have been doing a lot of work for the railways. These guys, Paul and Ray (Ray's my Dad) have never actually done any work for us.' (There were fourteen kilometres spread out over three packages put out for tender at the same time.) 'This is a large job for people unknown to us, Silver,' he continued. 'So, even though you guys are more expensive, we could probably still give Ray and Paul one of the packages and give you guys the other two.'

I was sitting beside Silver when he replied, 'Ah, Arty that all sounds good and I appreciate it, but we're just so busy I don't know if we'd be able to service you guys..'

Arty said, 'Yeah, fair enough, I might just give these other guys all three packages then.'

The money that Silver made from that job paid for all the money that he'd tipped into Paul Cameron's company. To his credit Paul Cameron called me the next day to congratulate us on getting the job and said he hoped it all went well. He smelt a rat but he didn't say anything. He knew there was nothing to be gained by going on about it. That's how he is. He's a smart guy, and it was a laugh because he told everyone he'd opened the 'Paul Cameron Investigation'. He said, 'Something's going on and I'm going to get to the bottom of it.' He never did, and about three or four years later I told him what had really happened. We're still friends today, do heaps together, and we still laugh about the Paul Cameron Investigation.

That job ended up taking about six months to complete. Over that time, we probably put about three hundred thousand in the bank because we actually did the job ourselves labour-wise. It was the first job we actually quoted on, and became the principal contractor for. That started a whole new world for me. From that time on all I used to do at night was look at tenders and priced jobs. That was after driving every day back and forth from Brisbane to Warwick, almost two hours each way.

About three months after getting that job I picked up another one out at Thornlands, a two hundred-thousand-dollar retainer wall for a civil company. From there it just started to roll on for us. Silver, who we were so close with all those years and who we did so much work for, and who opened the door for us, lost every Queensland Rail job to us over the next four years. He quit his job with Paul Cameron after the Warwick job and we're still good friends today, but we dominated the fencing industry with Queensland Rail for four or five years, and the fencing industry generally in our area for the next eight years.

Dad was great; just a really, really hard worker. He was always on the tools, not really into business and growth. In business I had to drag him every step of the way because all he really wanted to do was go to work and make his money and go home. However, he'd do whatever was necessary because, although he didn't really want to grow the business, we got on very well and enjoyed working together.

That was a mind-blowing introduction to business. By the time we'd finished the Warwick job we probably had about half a million dollars in the bank. That increased over the next twelve months of working, finding more jobs, and putting more money away.

LESSONS LEARNED

I started another company called Advantage Fencing, and leased a big place for twenty-five thousand a month at Brendale on the north side of Brisbane. I put in a whole lot of infrastructure and fabrication sheds in the back and, within about two months, I was broke.

I had no money left and it was a big lesson in cash flow. Although we owned all our own equipment, trucks, diggers and so on, I'd over-extended ourselves. We had too many projects going on, we had to buy too much material, we had way too many accounts outstanding, and wages were massive.

Working in construction, the best case scenario is that you get paid thirty days at the end of the month. If the invoice is missing just one thing, or is late by a day, it'll be pushed out another thirty days, and then another. Before we knew it, we had a million dollars owed to us, and they were out to sixty or ninety days. I was struggling, back to robbing Peter to pay Paul, except this Paul wasn't getting paid. Twelve months later we'd traded through that and worked our way back up, learning so much along the way. It was a massive learning curve for me.

Over the next eight years there were thousands of stories like that. We probably had about a hundred staff at any one time throughout the life of that company. To give you a helicopter view, I put in a powder coat plant, a fabrication plant, three chain wire machines which were from the States, each around a hundred and fifty thousand dollars. We were able to churn out thirty kilometres of chain wire a week. It had a massive impact on the fencing industry here in Queensland and that's what I was looking to do: take over the fencing industry in this state.

The problem was that I made way too much noise doing it. Everyone could see what I was up to and I didn't care. That was another huge lesson I learned. I wasn't aware that there were plenty of people and companies around with much deeper pockets. Suddenly, I had three chain wire machines and then all the other chain wire companies pulled their prices down dramatically, creating a price war. They were even prepared to work for nothing for twelve months to put me out of business.

We endured that for a couple of years by pricing any large chain wire jobs so that we won them, then supplying the chain wire to ourselves. It was hard for the opposition to compete with that.

After about five years, things had stabilised for us and we were winning large government contracts all over Queensland. We were going well. We decided to take on yet another business.

There was a gentleman that I was chasing after, Graham Woods, who used to be Natural Areas Co-ordinator for Brisbane. I was introduced to him by Paul Cameron, and Graham was sharing an office with Campbell Newman at the time.

I really wanted Graham to come and work for me. Advantage Fencing was thriving and there was a specific type of fencing put around natural areas in Brisbane called welded rail. It's a post and rail fence and you can see it all around our parklands to keep the four wheel drives and motorbikes out.

We were doing tens of kilometres of it when Paul Cameron came to me with an idea. Welded rail is labour intensive. Normally, you'd have to cut a rail and place it in the post and weld it in there. It takes a long time to do and is very expensive for the council. Paul had this scheme to have a pleat that looks like a rhino horn, weld it to the post, and then the rail runs straight past the post and they're welded. It serves the same purpose at half the price and twice the profit.

Paul floated it to us to see if we would back him on the idea but his track record with us definitely ruled that out. My old man was even more insistent that we didn't touch it, so Paul took the idea to another company, Northside Fencing. That was run by a guy called Mark Dowse, who was a bigger rogue than Paul. The deal was that Paul was to get a royalty on each of the rhino pleats they used.

Northside are then doing tens of kilometres of fencing and Paul's not getting a thing. He certainly jumped into bed with the devil there. It's a funny thing. Paul Cameron's a bit of a rogue and as much as he goes around trying to catch people, more often than not he ends up being caught. We laugh about it continuously. He works for me now, by the way.

Back to the story: After a year, Mark still hasn't paid Paul, so he's brought the idea back to us to reconsider. Well, now it's a proven product and easier to convince the old man that it would work. The deal was the same, two dollars a pleat to Paul.

Mark was still in the background; he'd spent a load of money on marketing but not much more. Rather than letting Mark know that we were going to do anything, we had a lawyer put a trademark on the name — something Mark hadn't done. So the tens of thousands of dollars that Mark had spent on marketing belonged to us now. We owned the name and if he wanted to use it he'd have to pay us a fee. We all look back and laugh at that too, but Mark was really angry at the time.

That sort of fell into our laps. We had a bit of fun with it more than anything. It was a little bit of a gee-up to get back at Mark because he's always been the conman around. He'd caught me a couple of times along the way as well. That's just what he does, and he'd do it again in a heartbeat. I tell you, I could call up any one of those guys, and there are hundreds of them, and we'd just look back and laugh at all those games. Then we'd look at what we might be doing next and get to it. There are no hard feelings, it's business, it's fun.

Anyway, back to Woodsy (Graham Woods) in the Brisbane City Council. From when we took over this rhino business, ninety percent of the work was supplied by him. He was respected by everyone in the Council, he was respected by his peers, and he was respected throughout the whole industry and also worked alongside Campbell Newman.

So this was the guy I wanted to come work for us and to run this rhino company that we'd discovered was going to be so great. At that time, Graham was Natural Areas Co-ordinator and he looked after all the rangers within all the natural areas. It was in all the natural areas that we wanted to fence with our product.

I wined and dined him for about twelve months. I took him to the races, and I took him out on the town. Finally, I was able to get him to come and work for us by creating a new company called Ryno, putting one third of it into Woodsy's name. Money wasn't the thing for him, but he'd recently split up with his wife and he had a young son. The way I brought him in was to tell him that it was fine that money wasn't the big thing for him, but didn't he want something more for his son's future? Take a third of this company's future and move forward. I told him that I thought council was a great job, but it's for people who can't do any better than that, and he had a lot more potential. So he came on board and worked for us.

Graham came on board about five years in to Advantage Fencing, and helped manage that company, at the same time setting up Ryno Fencing. I must say, for the first twelve months he was absolutely useless. He was just a dead weight, and I was thinking that he might have been a mistake. He'd been in government for ten years, not in business. It took those twelve months to get him to understand what we were doing and what we were trying to achieve.

I reflect on Woodsy a lot throughout my whole business life and probably use his name a lot. Some of my greatest lessons in life have come from Graham Woods. He's probably one of the smartest guys I know. He's always calm, he's respectful of others, and anyone who respects everybody the way that he does automatically gets respect in return. He treats absolutely everybody the way he wants to be treated no matter who they might be. He's the kind of person that you automatically love the day you meet him, and I'm lucky to have him as a good friend.

Another big thing I've learnt along the way is that you become an average of the main five people that you hang around. If you surround yourself with great people, you can't help but have them rub off on you. But the biggest thing I ever learned from Woodsy is to treat people the way you want to be treated, treat everyone equally no matter who they might be and they will respect you.

When Woodsy first came to work for us, regardless of whether he was good at his job or not, we had a whole motley crew working for us. There were about one hundred people and there were all types, including bikies. The whole gamut of workers that you find in the construction industry. There were some angry personalities and some arrogant personalities — all sorts. Everyone talks to everyone differently and some don't like each other. But one thing I can guarantee is after Woodsy had been there for about a month, he was the one person in the company that everyone loved and everyone respected. If someone said something arrogantly or angrily to him, he would not react. He'd just leave it at that and say, 'fair enough', or 'whatever', and walk off.

After a month of bedding himself in he'd say, 'Hey mate, I don't like the way that you speak to me, and I make a point of never speaking to you like that, so I think it would be good if we could just respect one another.' He got it to a stage where everyone could point to him and say, 'That guy gets respect because he shows respect and doesn't react to others' personalities.'

About four years after Graham started, Advantage Fencing went into liquidation. At that point we'd spent a lot of money in another industry, insulation, when the government was spending five billion dollars on it as a stimulus package. We spent a massive amount on it. We bought thirty trucks, we bought all these machines, we had a hundred guys out there and, when they switched it off, everything that we'd bought was worth nothing. We pretty much lost everything we had.

That was bad enough but, about six months after that happened, there was a bit of a chain reaction. A lot of the cash we used to get the insulation company going came from Advantage Fencing, so it was the taxation that pushed us into liquidation for the money that we owed the ATO. We were actually paying them off at the time and not missing a payment, so a lot of the pain that resulted from the insulation industry, a lot of that money that we lost, became unpaid tax — creating a domino effect.

We got pushed into liquidation by the ATO and the main reason we got pushed was because of the ATO's reaction to Paul Hogan telling them to basically stick it. When Hogan fought them and won, they had egg on their faces. From then, all deals with everyone were off. No one was allowed to pay off their overdue taxes. Advantage Fencing was taken to the Federal Court and liquidated for the million dollars we owed the ATO. Money we were faithfully paying off.

Ryno Fencing was a different company running concurrently. It was set up with me owning one third, my Dad a third, and Woodsy a third. Dad and I were partners in Advantage Fencing so, when that fell over, I gave my third of Ryno to him. By this time, he was in his late sixties and that's way too late to start again. I also felt somewhat responsible, because all those years I'd been wanting to grow bigger and bigger and now the whole thing had fallen over. Ryno's still a thriving business, and they'll probably do well over twenty million this year.

While we were in the insulation business we had another company called High Tech Hydro Mulch. We had a big hammer mill to mulch paper, and then found another use for the mulched paper called hydro mulch. It was sprayed on the side of highways and anywhere else they take the grass off. It's just mulched up paper with grass seed and water to basically spray grass.

That was a fairly successful company too. Woodsy and I were partners in that one, so it was something going on the side when everything fell over with Advantage. I also gave my half of that to Dad. He sold it two years later for six hundred thousand dollars. That helps me sleep at night.

I came out of all that with a little bit of money and invested it in a cafe with my wife Teena. It only lasted about six weeks and then we closed the doors. It was like a playland café, a huge place with dodgem cars and all sorts. It just seemed to be the rage at the time.

Teena had been wanting to build it for years so when Advantage folded I thought I'd try something new, although I built it more for her than myself.

As far as the business was concerned, I asked her to do two things. Firstly, not to employ any family, because she was all for giving her cousins and aunts jobs. I don't like employing family because I feel uncomfortable asking for my pound of flesh. I'm a bit of a perfectionist and I like things to happen my way because it works. It may work other ways too, I don't know, but I know the way I do things works and I like to stick to that. The other thing; I was to be in charge. My wife is a lovely person but she can't handle confrontation at all. She just melts, and that's not a good personality for heading up a business.

I insisted on those two things, because if we were going to borrow four hundred thousand dollars for this project I wanted it to work, otherwise I'd rather go and do something else. She agreed to those two stipulations, although she did get upset. It wasn't quite what she had in mind.

It never turned out that way. Her cousins were there, her aunties were there, and I had to say, 'No! No! No!' We were turning over seventeen thousand a week and going backwards. It could have been a great business but we were going backwards and we had to close the doors. We were only operating for around eight weeks and, if we had stayed at it for one more day, we wouldn't be married today, I guarantee it.

We could never work together again. It's never going to happen. When that failed I went up north and found a job on the mines and worked up there for twelve months. I actually worked for Ryno. I was back on the tools, but I'd help price the jobs, find the jobs to do, and I'd help win the projects for them. Then I subcontracted to them.

I just didn't like being away from home. I missed my children and I wanted to find something closer to home. Initially, I think I went up there and did the twelve months on the tools for a little bit of time out, for some quiet time where I was no longer responsible for others. It can really be taxing. For the past ten years I'd always been responsible for so many other people's incomes and families. When the money stops, everybody gets angry with me. It doesn't matter whose fault it is or what happens, it doesn't make any difference.

And strangely enough, that's when the training started.

THE WAY IT WORKS

A good way to get to know someone is to take a look at the people they surround themselves with and see if any of them have been around for longer than twelve months. That says a lot about a person. They may come across as being successful, say all the right things and seem to be doing all the right things, but if you take a look at their past and find they've got no long-term friends, I think that tells you little bit about them.

I had just recently started a new company and, looking for salespeople, I presented to nine guys who've have worked for me in the past. Seven of them signed on again. I don't like burning bridges. I ask the best from people and, if I don't get it, I don't necessarily keep them around. But I don't burn bridges.

So, there I was working at the mines for about twelve months and also working for Queensland Rail. It was twenty-eight days on, then seven days off. But I was contracted to companies up there so I'd only be home for a few days before I'd have to go up there again. I really hated it, but I'd had a great company fall over and had to do something to support my family. I just got on with things.

Looking back, the failure of my company hit me really hard. It had a massive impact on me. I worried about the stigma of being involved with that failure, I worried about my family who had grown accustomed to living very well over the years, and it's hard to pull back from that.

I can guarantee that my family don't really feel the blows of what goes on at work. I don't like to take that home. Neither do I ever want them to go without. It's important to minimise work problems and shield those I love from fallout. I usually put my phone on silent at nights and don't answer it on the weekends. I went through a phase of throwing my phone in my undies draw to hide it there so I couldn't even see it. I'm still a bit like that today. People get angry with me and label me an arse a lot for not answering my phone or checking my calls, but I go at a thousand miles an hour and, like everyone, I need downtime.

Up north, I was very down for a while. I felt like a drone, but strangely happy to be so. In a sense it was refreshing, to be working back on the tools, out on the site, and not worrying about anybody else. I still had a team of guys up there but it was very small after what I'd been used to for the past eight years. I now only had seven. I was no longer looking to grow any large business or anything like that. It was just hand to mouth. I just wanted to earn a living for a while.

So even though I was up there to zone out, do a job and put food on the table, I couldn't help myself. Another mine was being built a couple of hours' drive away, so I chased after and won the job. It was going to be a massive job. Despite wanting to stay small and stay under the radar, I couldn't help but go after it.

Although we got that job, we ended up pulling out of it because the mine we were working on just became too high maintenance and I thought that the next one would become just the same. Next thing we rolled straight into a Queensland rail job up there when I won a contract for about fifty kilometres of stock fence. It was the only fence on the railway sites but it was a massive, massive job and it was a challenge. So much for zoning out.

Then, one day when I was up there, Teena rang and said, 'Billy has asked if you're dead.' He was our youngest son and about three at the time. I laugh about it now, but it was a turning point for me, there's more to life than work and I desperately needed to find something closer to home.

While I was up there, my old mate Paul "Rogue" Cameron called me. He'd bought a half a million-dollar rail stud machine for putting in guard rail. He'd also bought a truck and invested eight hundred thousand dollars into this guard rail company, but he had no work.

There was thirty kilometres of guard railing to be done in Brisbane and he asked if I'd come on board with him and help him chase after it. Thinking it was a good opportunity to come home, I brought my guys back to Brisbane. There was a catch. My guys had to be pre-qualified in road construction to get pre-qualified for Main Roads and be allowed to do guard rails.

I had this friend Leo, originally a builder from Melbourne. After a failed marriage where he lost everything, he was in Brisbane to start again. He's such a character, he could write a book of his own.

Leo built a wine bar from literally nothing. At the time, he was living at his brother-in-law's place and sleeping on the floor. He had no money, no car, nothing. He came up with a concept to build a bar, took the idea to an accountant who liked it, and asked him who might be keen to invest in it.

He started using the accountant's boardroom for all his meetings, got it off the ground and did a great job. After twelve months that business fell over, so he started another one which also fell over. He learned a bit from those ventures, and now he's going really well in his own construction company. He also worked in my fencing company which is how I met him. In the end, I didn't have enough work for him and that's when he went into his wine bar.

We remained friends throughout that time and one day I was in his bar when he told me how he'd just got his diploma in building again. There were different rules from Victoria to Queensland and he needed a diploma in building to get his builder's licence back. He mentioned that he'd met this guy who was in some way working for the government who had helped him.

I had no idea how these things worked and I was happy for Leo at the time. But, a couple of months later, when I needed to get my guys pre-qualified, I called Leo and asked for the diploma guy's number. 'No worries,' he said. 'I'll call him for you.' Within minutes he rang back. 'Hey Paul,' he said. 'I've got a great deal for you. Not only is he going to do it for nothing, but you're going to get four thousand dollars a guy as well!' Now Leo gets into some pretty dodgy stuff. 'Hang on Leo, that doesn't make any sense,' I replied. 'I've got a lot of guys and that's a lot of money. I don't mind paying for my qualification, mate.'

Leo explained that it was all above board, so that night I got on the Internet and studied it up. To my amazement it was all true! Leo had an RTO (Registered Training Organisation), and this scheme was a federal incentive. It's still the same now, for anyone who does a Certificate III or Certificate IV the federal government will give the employer a four-thousand-dollar incentive. At the time, there was also twelve thousand dollars per student from the state government for every student that completed their Certificate III for the RTO.

So this guy was going to get twelve grand for each of the guys I'd had working for me for eight years and I'd get four grand too. I'd trained these men and worked with them for all those years, so they knew what they were doing. They just didn't have a piece of paper. It didn't take me long to realise I was in the wrong industry.

Over the previous ten years, all I'd done was train my own guys. I'd consistently had a big team and a massive turnover so this was a very, very easy progression for me. I'd never considered myself a salesman in my whole life, the limiting belief is that a salesman is like a real estate agent, a used car salesman, or someone selling snake oil. We're taught very young not to trust a salesman, so I never would have liked to think of myself as one. Things were about to change.

Leo had organised a meeting with John, the RTO owner, where I suggested that, rather than sign my guys up, why didn't I work for him? I was really keen to become a trainer, and told him so. I thought that I could get a job for a few grand a year and, at the same time, help others by adding value to their lives. I saw it as a fantastic opportunity for me because I was at a stage in my life where I wasn't worried about making pots of money. In fact, I wasn't worried about anything except supporting my family and doing something good for the community.

The horrific crash of my business had humbled me. I couldn't stop thinking about all the people who'd depended on me for so many years, needing a roof over their family's heads and food on the table. The time I'd spent away on the tools had given me time to think. I think I'd been searching for a new and worthwhile career for some time and had even considered the police service.

As much as I like to think that I'm hard with people, I was finding it more and more difficult to be tough, becoming a softer person as time went by, and I wasn't unhappy about that. I guess the more you get to know people, the more you get to love them. I was feeling myself opening up to people more and more. I've always worn my heart on my sleeve and struggled keeping secrets. People don't have to wonder what I'm thinking.

Back to John. I met him and instantly sparked up a relationship with this guy. I absolutely love him, he's a great guy. He's a total control freak, the biggest control freak I'd ever met. He's very, very OCD. Everything's got its place and everything must be just so. If you're thirty seconds late for a meeting with John, the chances are he's not going to be there. He's already gone because you had your fucking chance and you blew it, so fuck off. That's what John would tell you. A really hard guy.

I loved him instantly. He's an extremely smart person — one of the most intelligent people I know. He doesn't sleep, and you're getting emails from him at two in the morning. There's so much energy about him and, just by being around him, you become energised yourself. I like to think you become an average of the main five people you hang around, so obviously it's a good idea to surround yourself with people who are smarter than you to lift your own average. John did exactly that for me.

When I told him I wanted to work for him as a trainer, he offered me a deal. If I did all my own sales and trained all my own guys, he'd give me fifty percent of the funding for each student. It seemed great. I was going to get six thousand dollars for each one of my guys that I trained. I would be training them in what they already knew because I'd already coached them. Brilliant.

Coming from the ground up in Brisbane's construction industry meant I knew everyone in it. John, however, had come up from Sydney and didn't know a lot of people, so he was keen to align himself with someone like me who could help his business grow. What I didn't know at the time was that John didn't even have a state contract for funding. The only way he could get that was with Industry Support, and the reason he was offering to pay my students and not himself was because he needed a Letter of Industry Support from me to apply for the funding.

The cheeky bastard had offered me a job that didn't exist, and that was clever because, within one week, I had around fifty Letters of Industry Support on his desk and we were ready to go.

With our Letters of Industry Support in hand, we applied to the state government while I did my Certificate IV in Training and Assessing. The certificate took me four weeks whilst working with John, supplying him with Letters of Support and applying to the state government to get our funding through. Once that was approved, we had to go around and do an enrolment with all our students — by then it was over a hundred.

That first month we had our funding contract — a huge cause for celebration in itself, I was still questioning if it was all for real. It just seemed too good to be true. However, I was in up to my neck. If it didn't work out, I was screwed.

I wouldn't get any money from this venture until the new students had been trained. That would take three months. I had no back up if it fell apart. To keep my family going, I sold my truck, bobcat and all my tools.

At the end of each day, I'd think, *I hope this is going to work, I hope this guy's not ripping me off.* I'd only just met him, but I'd done my homework and, as much as it seemed too good to be true, and as much as my friends and family were telling me it was too good to be true and it's probably not going to happen, I couldn't see a flaw.

More than anything, I fell in love with the industry. I could see great opportunities for people to get a qualification in whatever they were doing. I'd never held a qualification myself and had been in the construction industry my whole life thinking that the only way to get one was to go to TAFE. I just didn't know there was another way.

As soon as we got our funding contract from DET (the Department of Education and Training), we had to get out there and start enrolling students. Then we had to do a half hour induction with each student and that was my introduction to training. The first day on the job is your opportunity to showcase the course training. While it's only an induction, there's so much that has to be explained. There's so much compliance in the training industry, so much the students have to be told, so many things they have to understand.

I inducted over a hundred people that month and then we had to wait six weeks for a registration number. After someone is enrolled, there is a six week wait for a registration number for them. Once that comes through, the training can start.

Financially, I was done. By the time we got to my first payment, my money had completely run out. It was a fine line. But my first cheque after those three months of work was one hundred thousand dollars, and after that the money continued to roll in each month.

At the time I didn't see it, but I was so well set up for this business. My experience, my contacts, and my people skills. I just couldn't work out why I was so successful; it didn't make any sense to me. I think that's why I was having a little bit of a hard time trusting John. Everything seemed too good to be true and it felt like he was blowing smoke up my arse. He was delighted with my success and kept telling me how well I was going. I'd never done sales in my life and he puts me in a sales role, telling me that I was the best guy he'd ever seen. To me, it was ridiculous and a little embarrassing.

When I think about it, I'd been in training for that role all my working life. I can see that clearly now, some five years down the track, but I couldn't see it at the time. A couple of months into it, John was employing more and more trainers to keep up with my sales. I trained my own guys for around six months, but then John made me the sales manager. Every weekly meeting John would make me feel really uncomfortable saying, 'I'd just like to stop and thank Paul for what he's done for us because without him this wouldn't have happened.' To me, it wasn't as if I was doing anything extraordinary or unusual, I was just being me. I was just doing standard, run-of-the-mill stuff, I was just in the lucky position of knowing the local construction industry.

I didn't think of myself as a salesman, nor did I think of my role in the industry as selling. Everyone needs a qualification in whatever they're doing, it just doesn't make any sense for them not to have a qualification, and it wouldn't make any sense for them not to want it. So to me it wasn't really a sale, it was just a truth well told — me explaining it to them correctly. What I've learnt since then is that the best salesman on the planet isn't seen as a salesman. If you're seen as a salesman, you've blown it. And in our case, we weren't selling anything anyway, we were giving it away. But there were a whole lot of guys in the industry who were struggling and couldn't even give it away.

There are five percent of people on the planet who have a natural ability for sales. They just have it, whereas the other ninety-five percent would have to be trained to get it. Most people can learn it, but it's all in the little things — the tonality, body language and rapport.

You won't get anyone to believe in what you're selling them if you don't believe in it yourself. It was something I had naturally but I hadn't known it. Jordan Belfort had it too, that's why he was so successful and why I brought him in. Like me, in the beginning, he didn't know why he was successful. He couldn't work it out. That's what the movie was based on; working out what people said that worked, what didn't work, and what's the right script, the correct energy, the positivity, tonality and timing.

Once his people learnt how to do what he was doing naturally, his whole company exploded, and it just took off. It wasn't any different for me. Things were happening for me that weren't happening for others and I went on a crusade to find out why. When I did begin to discover why, when I was reading about what was happening and why, it really excited me.

The hardest weakness to kill is the one you can't see. In sales, if you don't know what's going on, you're fumbling around in the dark as you're trying to connect the dots. That's incredibly frustrating. Whereas, the more you realise why something works, the more you're able to polish and get better at it.

It doesn't change who you are, what you're about. Your core values don't change. Your ability to understand yourself and what makes you tick just makes you a better salesperson. When I hire salespeople, I've found that ninety percent of them are lunatics, and that's been an education in itself. The type of people I would employ don't generally make good salespeople because they've got the wrong personality traits. To me, that's the hardest part about running a sales team — finding the right people.

I struggle running a sales team because salespeople are generally liars. You can't believe a thing ninety percent of them say. They give figures that never pan out and, if I still drank, they're not the sort of people I'd be having an afternoon beer with. A lot of them can be whoever they need to be at that particular time and, in short doses, they can be quite successful because the person they're selling to doesn't have the opportunity to figure out who they're dealing with.

I can't stand that type of personality. I can't stand a dishonest person. And because of the type of person I am, I can't help calling them on it. I can't stop myself from telling them to stop bull-shitting me. Inevitably, I have a personality clash with those people, and any one of my sales people would tell you that we don't always get on the best because of it. I get upset with their bullshit numbers and their bullshit stories. I'm not saying that all salespeople are like that but a great many are.

When we decided to bring Jordan in and really grow the business, we also brought in another person, already here in Australia, with his own large sales team of fifty guys. I didn't get on with any of those guys. From day one, I thought; *What? Who are these people?* Just like in the movie when Jordan's got a roomful of crazy people, that's exactly what it was like. We had a room full of insane guys, all different, but the one thing they had in common was that they were all relentless. When they're talking to someone they just keep chipping away and would keep coming back. They never take 'no' for an answer. I hate that.

Up until the time Jordan came on board, I brought my guys in for training every morning at five o'clock. At first, they hated it. For an hour I'd do skills training, not only about the industry and about compliance, and the right guys for the right jobs, but also about sales and what to do with body language, tonalities, scripting, and so on, just to make sure they're were on the right track, and to make sure they're going out with the right attitude.

When Jordan came on board, all that went out the window. We ended up with a big room full of these sales guys and I wouldn't want to deal with it because I'd just get angry talking to them. It was ruining things, so I distanced myself a bit from the sales side of it at that point.

But I'm getting ahead of myself. Let's go back to when John was my CEO and I was the Sales Manager. I stayed with him for twelve months and, as the business grew and grew, we moved offices twice, had thirteen hundred students, and everything was going fantastically well.

Remember that John was an absolute control freak — a great attribute in the RTO world where everything has to be structured and just so. Mistakes shouldn't be made in the training industry. But John controlled everything and micro-managed everything to death.

We'd agreed to go halves in a new office in Redcliffe, but it did need some work so my guys and some of his worked on the place for two weeks. I should have seen the writing on the wall then because John wouldn't let me pay for anything and, when I did, he'd give me the money back. He did have plenty of money, and he was making more money out of the deal than me, so I thought, *fair enough*. It was also his RTO from the start and I thought that he wanted a bit of separation and to regard the office and building as his.

John was one of those guys I mentioned earlier, someone who seemed to know nobody for more than twelve months. I'd certainly never met anyone that had. He had a long list of enemies and no long-term friends. I could see that every relationship was short-lived with John, for some reason or another. He's a bit of a loner, and in the back of my mind I was wondering when I would also be dispensed with. By then, we'd become very close and worked tightly together.

I'd had this girl, Charlie, working for me for six months into the twelve-month period. When I'd had to go around and do all the enrolments and inductions on site, I employed Charlie to do those inductions for me. She was already working for the apprenticeship centre so I poached her to come over to us. She was a trustworthy person and a great worker.

One day, when I was leaving at 2am the next morning to do some enrolments in Rockhampton, and because Charlie was going to be at work until five that afternoon, I left her the key to the building. The only two people who had a key were him and I because John didn't trust anyone.

Even so, I had no idea how big a deal the key issue was, it had never come up before. After I'd left to go home for a sleep that afternoon, John came in, saw Charlie and said, 'Okay Charlie it's time to go, I'm locking up now and going home.'

It was about four o'clock so she said, 'No it's okay John, I've got another hour's work to do,' He told her she'd have to leave because he was locking up. 'That's okay John,' she told him. 'I've got a key.'

He exploded, 'What? What do you mean you've got a fucking key?' He confiscated the key, kicked her out, and then he sent an email out to everyone saying that there had been a breach of the key protocol and he's got the locksmiths in to change all the locks in the building.

I didn't discover any of this until two the next morning when I woke up ready to drive to Rocky. There wasn't just one email, there were a bunch of them, so I decided I couldn't head off, I'd have to go into the office and sort the thing out. He hadn't invited me to the meeting, I found out about it from Charlie. I went in fifteen minutes late. Everyone's there and Charlie's in tears.

I really didn't get it and going into that meeting was probably the worst thing I could have done. Since then I've learnt about personalities and that you never pick a fight with a high D, the bullies, you stand up to them but you never pick a fight. Another thing with a high C, a high compliance person, is that you never prove them wrong because that type of personality doesn't like it. You learn all about these personality traits in sales and I wish I'd known about it back then. I'll go into it a bit more later.

So I turned up at the office and find all the sales guys and the trainers are there. It suddenly occurred to me that this was a bit of a set-up and that John didn't really need me anymore, he just needed all the guys that I'd brought in. Mind you, the sales guys were all working for me.

At the start, I was supplying the training and sales and we were going fifty percent in the funding we got. He was getting his fifty percent just from running the RTO and the compliance side of it. The guys worked for me and that's how the whole thing grew to where it was.

I was suddenly thinking that he might be seeing more money for himself if I wasn't there. If he just paid those guys directly, I wouldn't get my cut which wasn't actually a lot at the time because we'd spent money on moving, sales drives, and generally growing the business.

'What are you doing here?' John said, as I walked into the meeting. 'You're supposed to be in Rocky.'

'I am meant to be,' I replied. 'But I'm not going anywhere when there's trouble going on.

'Trouble?' he said, 'What? There's no trouble, what are you talking about?'

'Well, why is Charlie in tears then?' I asked. 'If there's no trouble, then why is Charlie crying? Obviously there is a problem and I think we should sort it out.'

That was probably the worst thing one could do, to have it out in front of everyone. He's not only a control freak, he's been karate training for the past thirty years. He's not a weak guy, he's a stand-up-stick-your-chest-out sort of guy.

The writing was on the wall. He offered me a different package, one where I could keep my sales guys but he would keep my trainers. I'd get twelve hundred dollars per enrolment, which probably wasn't a bad deal because I still would have made around seven hundred thousand a year. But it was the principle. We'd had a deal and how many more times would it change if I took his new one.

I thought about it for a few days before seeing him. 'Thanks John,' I told him. 'I appreciate the offer but it's probably not for me.' At that, he became very, very angry at me. He couldn't believe I was saying no. 'I'm sorry John,' I added. 'I just like to think that I'm worth more money than that.'

I must admit, I'd become rather cocky over the past twelve months and it was only a year back when I would have worked for anything. Actually I'm still not sure whether it was about the money or the principle, ego, or what.

I put my hand out to shake his hand and said, 'Look mate, I appreciate the offer but I don't think it's for me.' He hesitated for a bit and then shook my hand.

'When you go out into the real world,' he said, 'and you tell people what you turned down here today, they're going to laugh in your fucking face.'

'We'll just see how we go,' I replied. 'I just think I'm worth more money.' That did it. Charlie and I found our stuff dumped at the door.

I know that when I left, John's sales dropped right off and he had to find five guys to replace Charlie and I. They were also doing only half of what we were doing which made me feel good about myself. And I never saw the last payment I was owed — around two hundred thousand. When I asked him for it, he told me to go fuck myself. I still had to pay my sales staff, so at the end of that twelve months I was back to where I started, but with a lot more knowledge.

I was feeling confident. I wasn't concerned, I was positive, and I could see a brighter future. At that point I was thinking that he'd probably done me a favour. I felt that it was a financial setback but, overall, he'd given me a huge opportunity. Only last year I took him out for breakfast and thanked him for getting me into the industry in the first place. I told him that I had no hard feelings at all. He's the smartest guy I know and he gave me this amazing opportunity.

The first thing I did was to get a business broker to see what RTOs were being sold. I had to get my own thing up and running — something both exciting and scary. I only had fifty thousand in the bank so I sold my car, my boat, and a motorbike for the start-up funds and to keep us going. And that's how Face-to-Face began.

At the time of the split from John, I was in the middle of negotiations with a company called Murphy Pipe and Civil and they were doing a billion dollars' worth of business in Australia alone. I was having talks with the superintendent on the site of one of their gas pipe projects, and he'd given me an opportunity to do a presentation to the company's board of directors. They had a two hundred-million-dollar job about to start out west with three hundred full-time workers and I wanted to provide all their training. Everyone was eligible for qualification and I would get ten thousand dollars for each of them.

I could offer them absolutely anything. If they needed fire extinguisher training, spill kit training, four-wheel drive training — anything. I'd do all that for nothing if they would give me the qualification training. If I got myself five trainers they could provide accommodation and a training room.

The day after I picked up my things from the door of John's office, I put together a powerpoint presentation. The following day, I did the pitch to this high-powered board of directors with Charlie. I was incredibly nervous. I'd never spoken to anyone of that calibre in a company like that before and didn't know what to expect. These days I do.

I couldn't have done it without Charlie. She is fantastic and very confident, whereas I am very shy and quiet. We got through our presentation and they loved what we had to show them. I couldn't believe it, once again it all seemed too good to be true. These funded qualifications had been around for some time in Queensland and they'd never heard of it.

They've got managers who look after everything including training and they knew nothing about it. The international director said to me, 'Paul, the other day I got an email saying I'd won all this money in the lottery and I knew it was a scam. I've got the same feeling about this. Are we even going to see any of this money you're promising?' He was referring to the four thousand dollars per trained worker they'd get as an incentive from the federal government. With three hundred guys to train they were entitled to one point two million dollars just for letting us come there. And they didn't have to pay us a penny because we were getting three million dollars from state funding.

On top of that, anyone doing a Certificate III on site was payroll tax exempt so there was another million dollar saving. They were going to add two million dollars to their bottom line, plus they'd get us for free so there was probably a five million dollar saving for them.

Their guys would get qualified and that's taking a headache away because on those sites everyone has to have a VOC (Verification Of Competency). For example, it doesn't matter if a guy drives one thousand kilometres to get to the work site, as the principal contractor you have to verify that the guy is capable of driving a car — you have to give him a test. The same thing goes for plant equipment, or whatever, everyone has to be VOC'éd as they come on site, so we took that pain away from them.

It was a no-brainer that it was going to be good for them and good for us. They loved it and they wanted to do it but it was an expensive project for us to get up and running. Once again I've got that three-month lag before getting a payment. I'd presented this without any funding in place — pretty much what John had done twelve months earlier with me. They wanted me on site in one week to start the training so it was a mad whirlwind of activity.

Paul (centre) pictured at the family home in Bracken Ridge in 1977 with mum, dad, and elder brothers Michael and Duane.

Paul in the mid-1970's.

Kids in the bath. Paul (centre) with brothers Michael, Duane and cousins.

Paul (centre) with elder brothers Duane (on left) and Michael (on right) in 1976.

Paul at pre-school in Bracken Ridge.

Paul (at age 12) getting tickled by mum.

Paul on his wedding day.

Paul Cameron, Jordan Belfort and Paul Conquest at a private cocktail party, Crown Casino, Melbourne, November 2014.

Wade Grundon presents Paul Cameron with a cheque in honour of receiving 'BD of the week' award on 6th February 2015.

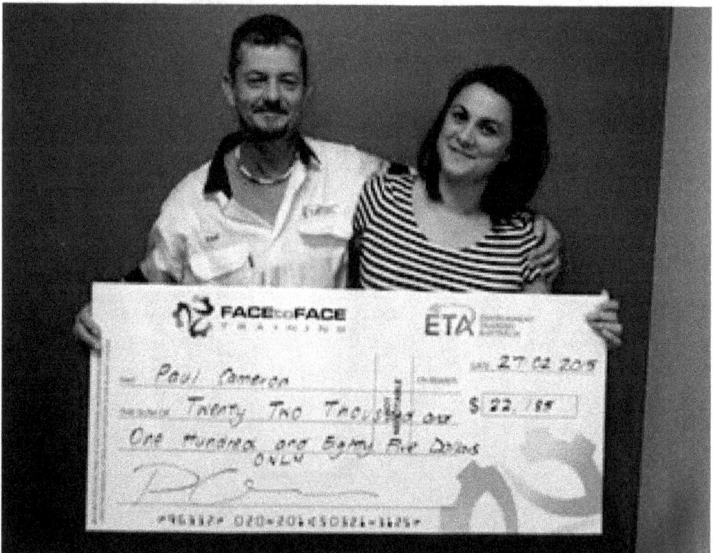

Paul Cameron and Charlie Tucker, pictured on 27th February 2015 with cheque to represent Paul Cameron's second 'BD of the week award'.

The meaning of training

The training industry was so attractive to me was because I thought it was the most powerful thing on the planet. I believe that training saves many, many lives.

I tell this story to all my sales guys. There's a famous photo taken when the Rockefeller building was under construction. It's of a bunch of workers sitting up on the girders eating their lunch. I have that photo on my office wall because it sums up training for me.

Back then it was accepted that one worker would die for every million spent on building a skyscraper, or a certain number would perish per floor. Lives would be lost so regularly that there'd be a line of workers waiting for someone to be killed, creating a job vacancy. In a race to get the building up, there were no safety precautions at all.

Now, in the construction industry, the acceptable fatality level is zero. It took us a long, long time to get to that stage and now when people go to work, every one of them has the right to go home in the same condition they arrived. Those are the human rights we have these days, and it's not that long ago that things were so different.

Twenty years ago, I used to go to work on a construction site in my singlet and thongs, and that was okay. We've come so far to get to where we are now. It hasn't been an evolution; it's been more of a revolution. Now, the only way that we can ensure that someone goes home every day is to first make sure they're competent in whatever it is they might be asked to do. And the only way to make sure someone is competent, because them saying they are is not enough, is to have some sort of formal competency, and to have them undergo some sort of formal test to show their competency. So the revolution we've undergone to ensure everyone goes home at the end of the day couldn't have taken place without giving everyone that competency. If someone gets hurt, someone's accountable because whoever asked that person to do what he was doing should have first checked to see that he was competent.

For an entrepreneur like me, someone who cares about safety and competency, this is the best industry on the planet. It can only keep growing, because we can never say, 'Well, you know, this is all getting very expensive, I think we should take a step back and start putting money before safety again.' We can never do that and what's the bet that in ten years you're going to need a qualification just to drive a truck. The most dangerous thing anyone does is drive to work every day, so why shouldn't our truck drivers have qualifications? That qualification can't be from an employer because there would obviously be a conflict of interest there so it needs to come from a third party.

Every time a life is lost in the construction industry, everyone in the industry is affected. There's a moment of silence and, for the next few days, everybody reflects on what happened. Every time we lose someone we learn from it. You look at how you lost that person, and every construction industry across the country then puts things in place so that will never happen in our workplace again. If someone gets killed by a reversing truck because they didn't see it coming, then no one from then on would be allowed to reverse a truck on the work site without having a spotter behind him when there's no one else around.

Every construction site that loses someone can be closed down anywhere from a week to a year and everyone on that site needs to have access to counselling, so it's a really big thing when a life is lost. Whether the person is a close friend, or just someone working on the same site, it's horrible all the same and everyone in the industry feels it and shares the pain.

There's an art to changing the way people think about safety and training. It's the art of persuasion, the art of finding a way to explain something to someone to get them to consider doing something differently. My Dad never accepted the changes. He hated them. He thought it was a crock of shit. He hated wearing his work boots, and he was always looking for a way to get around the rules when we worked together. You're not allowed to use a nine-inch grinder on site any longer because there are so many injuries caused by them. You're now only allowed to use a seven and a quarter inch. He didn't want to use a seven and a quarter. 'I've always used a nine inch so that's what I'll use,' he said, 'Fuck that! Paul, you be lookout while I'm working and make sure no one's coming.'

We had so many arguments about those sorts of things. When I told him I was going into training and checking people's competencies and so on, he was retired, but he said, 'Well giving someone a qualification doesn't make them any smarter.' He didn't agree with it at all. He couldn't see the value in it. That's the evolution or the revolution that we're in; old school people and maybe sixty percent of the population still don't see the value in it. They don't understand, but when I tell the Rockefeller story it makes sense why we're doing what we're doing, and why it's so important. Not only do they not get it here in Australia yet, they don't get it all over the world. It's a worldwide problem.

If you want to get a qualification in America you've got to pay for it yourself. There's no funding for the requirements that you need. You just have to go out and get it and pay for it yourself. If you look at countries like China and India and others, they're still happy to just price human lives into a building. They're still using bamboo for scaffolding. Obviously, human life doesn't have the value there that it does here, but it will sooner or later.

We can't possibly send people out to work without checking that they're competent. Regardless of whether you're just checking them or assessing them, everyone needs it. The most valuable thing we have in the world is human life and we should be doing more to protect it.

At the beginning of my training career it was an awesome feeling knowing I was making hundreds of friends for life, day in day out. Not only was I helping to save lives, but just helping someone who has been working in the industry all their life to get recognition with a formal qualification that they can put up on their wall meant I'd made a friend for life. That's because it turns their life around. Suddenly, they can prove that they're competent, and they can get a better job off the back of that qualification. Even though they had the skills, they couldn't improve their work prospects until they got that qualification.

The other reason the training industry is so attractive to me is the delivery strategy that we put in place. For most people, the only way they could get a trade like building or bricklaying was to go to TAFE for block training at the same time as going to work. A person can now train through an RTO. The education system has been privatised.

This is exciting because although the TAFE system had a twenty to thirty percent success rate, not many people can release their guys for three weeks at a time to go to TAFE. Agreed, anyone doing a higher risk of injury job like electrical work or plumbing needs training before working. But where you have someone swinging a hammer, or laying bricks, it's more effective to train them on site.

Similarly, with something like plastering. What's the point of taking someone out of productivity for three weeks when they can be trained effectively and better on site? Often, when the guys are due to go off for training, the boss can't afford to let them go so it just doesn't happen. It's a massive problem in Australia, which means there are a lot of people working out there without any recognition through formal qualifications.

The business model we rolled out made such perfect sense. We would go out to a site and spend one hour per month with every student, one-on-one, face-to-face. In TAFE, you have a classroom full of people and you don't know who knows what or who's done what, where some guys might know everything while others know almost nothing, so you have to cover off on absolutely everything which is really inefficient. That's why it takes three weeks to cover it all. You're probably telling most of the guys in the room how to suck eggs. They've done all this stuff, they know it, they understand it, but it has to be covered for any who haven't had the experience.

The advantage with one-on-one is you start off with a one or two-hour conversation with the student, getting to know exactly what they've done and what they know. This is written down in an RPL kit (Recognised Prior Learning), and we then know what we have to cover with that student to get him where he needs to be. We get a one hundred percent outcome; we don't brag about getting thirty percent. That in itself is a much stronger business model than the current TAFE system. On top of that, there's not even any sales required because it's just the truth well told. If you explain to people what they need, how you're going to achieve it for them, and how it's better than the TAFE system that may not achieve it for them, you've got them.

What's so important in the training industry is that there are a lot of rules around the qualifications that a trainer must hold first. There are also rules around how long they need to have held that qualification, as well as strict guidelines around professional development that they must undertake every year to stay current. They also have to spend a certain amount of time in the field each year because things are always changing.

As an RTO, a register should be held for all of the above, and it has to be shown in an audit. We kept up with that one hundred percent even though it was an enormous job for us. I could see the importance of it and also knew that if we were going to grow hugely it would mean people would be looking over our shoulders. The fact that we were successful and stepping on toes in the industry meant that we'd be audited regularly and I wanted to be ready for it.

You can't possibly grow and not expect people to try to drag you back down, so we knew very well that all compliance had to be bulletproof, and that's exactly what it was. We made sure that the trainers were well trained, that they did have professional development, and that we had a continuous improvement register (there were so many different registers for those guys). Those were the rules that we were supposed to abide by and we did.

It's a very competitive industry and we were doing our job well. With everyone jumping on board with us, the other RTOs were hurting, so it was a weekly thing for us to answer questions from the department of education and from ASQA (Australian Skills Quality Authority) — the federal watchdog regarding formal complaints against us from our competition.

We got our fair share of questions because we were doing so well. When ASQA and the state regulator saw that we were doing a lot of work and that we were putting a lot of numbers through, it was obvious they were going to have a lot of queries. We were happy about that. We were making a lot of noise, people were looking our way, and we were making sure we got it right.

Then there's the students who want the qualification but don't actually want to earn it by putting in the work. They are trouble. Our call centres did surveys and found that ninety-seven percent of our students were satisfied. The other three percent were students who either didn't do the work, or didn't have the skills to get qualified. Some of those guys would try blackmail and threats, telling us they'd go to the DET and tell them we were dodgy.

The other large RTOs, the ones who were doing it right, weren't ones to complain to the department about us. It was the many smaller RTOs that felt pressure from us and therefore complained. We knew why, and I believe both DET and ASQA have a lot to answer for here.

If we were training people in the concreting industry, for example, one of our people would turn up to explain something to a student and they'd tell us that they'd had a salesperson from another RTO come out and give them both training and certification on the same day. And the salesperson wasn't even a concreter.

I strongly believe that the whole training industry here in Queensland needs cleaning up, but what happens is that a whole lot of RTOs which get audited over and over again do exactly the same stuff over and over, and nothing ever happens about it.

Yesterday, I heard an ad on the radio trying to get people to do a Cert III in Surface Extraction. A Cert III in Surface Extraction is a mining qualification, so if you work on a mine it would normally take two or three years to get that qualification. It may not take that long if someone's already spent a couple of years on a mine. In that case, one could get recognition of prior learning into that qualification, but you'd need that experience first.

On a mine, we're talking about two to four hundred tonne excavators and one hundred or two hundred tonne Moxy dump trucks for moving the stuff around. They're massive.

This RTO was advertising on the radio to do a Cert III in Surface Extraction in ten working days. They're targeting unemployed people, offering them the prospect of a job in the mines. There is no work in the mines at the moment. The mining industry in Queensland has gone for now, with thousands and thousands of people unemployed.

But the state government has still got a funding contract available to pay an RTO three thousand dollars per student to do a qualification in a Cert III in surface extraction, so they're advertising and bringing in these people to do the course in two weeks and they're showing them how to operate a little bobcat and a three tonne excavator. There's a huge amount expected in a mining qualification, so it's not a planned competency, it's actually twenty units of competency within the mining qualification and they're including an excavator ticket of competency. A person should have spent an extra three hundred hours on that excavator. It's called nominal hours, and every competency has nominal hours attached to it.

This particular qualification would have about twenty competencies that have to be passed. How could anyone do that in two weeks? It's simply not possible. But we've got training companies doing it in ten days and getting paid three thousand dollars by the state government. They're putting thirty guys a week through so they're making ninety thousand dollars a week with that particular qualification and people are walking away with a piece of paper which essentially belongs in the toilet. For one, they couldn't possibly know the material that they need to know to be competent in that area, and two, no one is ever going to accept it. You take that piece of paper to a mine and they'll laugh you all the way back to Brisbane.

This is what's happening right throughout the entire industry and it needs to come out. We were doing none of that. We became undone because we had Jordan working for us. It was a cover-up more than anything else, because as soon as someone in the industry makes a bit of noise, the government covers it up, which is exactly what they did with us. The media were talking about Jordan, but if they wanted to talk about the quality of training they would have come unstuck because there was nothing to prove wrong there. Later, we endured a four-week audit and they had nothing to show against us. And we never received a copy of that audit, but more on that later.

The funding contract was with DET. DET decided what funding each qualification would get and they do site visits to make sure all the training is being done correctly, the right supervisors are there, the right trainers, and so on. They write the funding rules that have to be abided by to be able to train students and then they audit against it. They're the funding provider and the state regulator. Then you've got the federal regulator which is ASQA who writes the whole training package. ASQA show you how many nominal hours must be attached to each qualification. It's a federal registration so each RTO has to be registered through ASQA; that's how you become an RTO.

In order to become registered, they first have to audit all the RTO's learning materials, all their assessment materials, and that has to match back to the government qualifications. All RTOs write their own training material, there's no set material to work with. Everyone writes their own and that's what makes one RTO much better than another. One might have material of a much higher standard, or material that is more user-friendly, or more informative. But first that all has to go through ASQA to get compliancy before registration can be obtained for that particular qualification. Once you do that, you apply for your SCOPE, they look at all your materials, policies and procedures, and then you're away — you're allowed to train.

The thing with ASQA is that in years gone by they would audit regularly when people asked for SCOPE, but because this whole industry has blown out and ASQAs so out of control, I could apply for SCOPE this week for five new qualifications and I'll probably have them by next week, and they wouldn't have looked at a damn thing. They give everybody a risk rating and it seems very easy to get a low risk rating. I could go and put a qualification on SCOPE, apply for it today, and I might have it next week. ASQA wouldn't have looked at it or have any idea of how I intend implementing it. In a week, I could be training with material that doesn't meet any requirements but which has the tick of approval. And now I'm giving out qualifications that are being nationally recognised across the country and being funded by DET. That whole system has now become industry standard because that's what everybody's doing. Someone sees someone else getting away with it, so then a heap of RTOs are jumping on that bandwagon and doing the same.

The only reason to get penalised for doing any of that is if you made a little bit of noise, like having Jordan Belfort come on board. At any time, I could show you our wall chart consisting of around thirty compliance people. I gave those people the power of our whole company. I said, 'You guys run the company,' because at the end of the day if we got caught doing something non-compliant, we may as well not have a company. It would be over. I told the compliance people, 'You guys have an open cheque book and you guys make all the rules and the rest of the company simply has to abide by them.' We were very careful with our organisational charts to make sure our compliance always came first.

∼

ASQA have more to answer for than anybody. They're the federal regulator on the quality of everyone's training material. They set the rules and standards. DET are supposed to audit people, but they only audit everything against the standards set by ASQA. The government has been talking about scrapping ASQA for the past few years but they keep extending their contract. ASQA are contracted to be the regulator and they keep talking about changing the system, but the government just keep giving them second chances.

I could talk for days about things that happen within the industry and the things that a lot of people get away with and have gotten away with over many years. There are more moves than a can of worms in this industry. It's so entangled and so many people are getting away with dodgy behaviour simply because companies aren't getting audited.

Then there are RTOs who are turning over in excess of three hundred million each year and they're up to far more dodgy things than we've ever been accused of.

There's another national funding model called Vet Fee-Help. It's ridiculous. There are RTOs around signing up hundreds of millions of dollars and getting extremely low completion rates.

The system is that you get paid before you actually do the training. You get paid up front by the government. I never wanted to get into it because I just don't think it's a smart business model. How could it possibly last? But that's our government; they've put in a model where the RTO actually gets paid before they provide the training. Theoretically, it's a loan, although the recipient doesn't have to pay it back until they're earning around fifty-three thousand dollars a year.

So salespeople went around demographically poor areas, targeting houses with overgrown lawns and unmotivated people who are never going to make that sort of money. They'd offer them the chance of getting a qualification and part of that offer was a free iPad. Now they've signed this person up for an eighteen-thousand-dollar qualification, given them a free iPad, and that person goes and hocks that iPad to get some cash, never having any intention of doing the course.

But the RTOs are getting paid for it. They're the people they're targeting and because it's an online qualification training costs are minimal. If that person never gets online, it's not their problem. They only have to give the person access to an online qualification and their job is done.

Last year they got caught out by 60 Minutes. They showed what their sales people were actually doing. On top of that it showed that when you sign someone onto a management type of qualification, they also have to pass an LLN which is a language, literacy and numeracy test before they are eligible to do it. The sales guys were doing it for them. They were standing at the front door doing the LLN test for the potential student. Hundreds of millions of dollars and it all got swept under the carpet — until now. Another company were doing the same sort of things but they were pulling in five hundred million. They're still around, they've just changed their name.

This is a fantastic industry and, done right, it's the best industry on the planet. But what's happening here in Australia is corruption on a major scale, and it's become industry-accepted.

THE IRISH

People aren't stupid. Companies know the difference between a good qualification and a bad one, and good ones are backed up by work experience. Generally, there's work history to back up a qualification. Holding a piece of paper with no work history isn't worth a great deal. There is still value and a market in doing it properly and giving someone a proper qualification with proper training that they earn. And, depending on which RTO provided it, the name of the RTO is also going to give it value.

Going back a bit to that Murphy job after John and I parted ways, the board wondered why they'd never heard of that training initiative before. Murphy Pipe and Civil had training managers who were supposed to look after training for the whole company and, supposedly, knew about it. They knew about it all right; they just chose to ignore it because there were people out there with their hands out doing back door deals. Needless to say, that middle management didn't like us being on site. The directors wanted us there, the guys onsite wanted us there, but everyone else in the office wasn't happy about us. Of course, people from the old guard got into trouble, and some lost their jobs.

The first day on site, we had forty people in a room who had never done any classroom-based training, or anything like it. Murphy's middle management had put together a massive list of things that we had to train them in. It was a huge spreadsheet of all the training they'd come up with and, to be quite honest, we didn't know much about any of it. We'd never trained anyone on a fire extinguisher or a spill kit, but it was day one and we had to prove ourselves. They'd also put some secret shoppers in the classroom to try to trip us up.

Charlie and I had put the training together and she'd come with me. To say I was terrified would be an understatement. My heart was racing, my voice was cracking, and I couldn't talk properly as I'm trying to train a room of forty Irishmen, and can't understand a bloody word they're saying. Charlie and I were so relieved to get through that first day.

The site superintendent was happy. He wanted the training and wanted it to work, so he told the secret shoppers to piss off. They weren't too happy about that. They pulled everything we said to pieces, so he pulled the secret shoppers out of the room and said, 'I want them here and the directors want them here so you can fuck off.' His exact words. That drove a wedge through the company between the three hundred Irishmen, us, and the rest of the company. It was tumultuous, with rumours going around about what we were doing and what we weren't doing, and all the dodgy work that was going on right through the company.

I put the fact that we got through that first presentation down to Charlie. She's a much stronger person, and a stronger personality than me. We were both there and we were both terrified but I believe she got us through it. That was day one on the job, but the second day didn't get any easier. Neither did the third day or the fourth day. Out in Wandoan, the middle of nowhere, every day we turned up to work and there would be another challenge.

We didn't have any money and we had five trainers out there to do plant training, one of whom was me. My trainers wouldn't do anything they didn't know anything about so, if there was anything they didn't know about, I'd have to do it myself. Middle management came and asked us for a vehicle pilot course the third day in to teach people to pilot a truck driver with oversize loads. They wanted to put twelve guys through this course. Who puts twelve of their guys through a course like that? It was unheard of, but that's what they wanted and they wanted it the following morning. They really hated us and regularly gave us the impossible.

That night, after a hundred phone calls, we found someone in Rockhampton who was able to do it. We flew him in and, after working until six o'clock that night, I had to pick him up from the airport at Roma, a three hour drive each way.

Arriving back at the site at midnight, I was shattered. Up at five the next morning, I did my day's work then drove him back to the airport to get him back home again. That was an average day out there for about six months. Day in and day out. Charlie cried every day because they put so much pressure on us. Making it work was our only priority. It was a fantastic opportunity with a billion-dollar company, and over the years there would be hundreds of millions of dollars of training to be done.

Charlie and I still laugh about the day I told her, 'Charlie you know what? This seems so hard now but I can guarantee that, give it a couple of years, we're going to look back on this and laugh so much. We're going to laugh about that time we were stuck out on site in the middle of nowhere to do all that training.' And it's true, we do look back and laugh. It's such a funny thing now.

It's hard for me to tell this story because it's hard to relate back to how bad it felt. I can't even get my mind around how bad it was being stuck out there in the middle of nowhere with all that pressure. There were many time I felt like chucking it all in. Many times. I have to admit that I had to hold back the tears out there as well. Every day was a new nightmare. Every day they'd come storming through the door. 'Alright guys,' they'd say. 'Today we need some competencies on graders. We've got a whole heap of grader drivers turning up and you need to train them.' We'd never driven a fucking grader before. We didn't know the first thing about graders. So we're out there acting as if we did. Worse, we didn't have the correct paperwork, so we had find somewhere to buy the paperwork. But, first of all, we'd have to find someone to borrow the money off to buy the paperwork to train the grader drivers. I was broke. I'd done all my dough with John.

Just to fill in, there are a lot of RTOs around with state funding that will do a partnership agreement. They'll allow you to use their funding if they can take thirty percent off the top and leave you with seventy percent. So I did exactly that with another particular RTO, but for them to take you on, you have to pay thirty thousand dollars up front, after which you can use their qualifications, resources and everything.

It was a great deal for this particular RTO because out of the three million dollars, they were going to make one million dollars just by collecting the paperwork from us. Mind, I still had to find the thirty thousand dollars they demanded up front.

It transpired that they didn't even have any resources. We'd paid the money, we were waiting out on site, and they kept promising it. Eventually, we realised that they didn't even have any so we had to go out and buy it. And, every time we trained or assessed, we had to go and buy the resources for that particular course.

At the same time all this was going on, I had another arrangement running in the background with another RTO called Face-to-Face. Purchasing an RTO requires consent from DET. The owner of Face-to-Face already had a DET contract, but didn't have the scope qualifications we needed. We agreed that I would purchase his RTO for two hundred thousand dollars once the appropriate scope was there.

We drew up a contract whereby the appropriate scope would be obtained and funding from DET with that scope would be secured. For that, he would get ten percent off the top until settlement which we estimated to take about six months. At that time, we also asked for DET approval, for which we estimated three or four months.

That was happening at the same time as we were using IPS and, about six months into our time out at Murphy's, we got our funding through scope so we changed it over to our own RTO, Face-to-Face, and paid only ten percent instead of thirty.

I bought Face-to-Face off Matt Rawlinson and, after about twelve months of trading, while it was still in his name and he was still receiving his ten percent, we were struggling to get him to settle because he found himself making so much money. Eventually, solicitors had to be involved and it cost us a fortune. Even in the very last month when it was finally meant to settle, he made it run two days over the month and scored another seventy thousand. He was very cunning. No sour grapes here though, everybody did well at the end of the day.

The Murphy project rolled on for twelve months, but I was only out there for the first six to get it going, and then I couldn't handle it anymore. I was over Murphys and, as we had our own RTO, and our own funding, I came back to Brisbane to grow the business rather than be out there at their beck and call. I put some other people out there in my place so we still honoured our agreement and we did everything that we said we would.

I learnt so much from that job. Obviously, I learnt classroom-based training by being chucked in at the deep end, and a lot more. At the time, I looked back twenty-five years at my time in the work force, getting around in shorts and thongs and nothing much really mattered in the way of safety. The work ethic was very strong back then and all you really cared about was getting the job done. Working on a site with three hundred Irishmen was like taking a step back to those times. There were fist fights all the time and it was crazy, but they were the hardest workers on the planet. Their whole ethos was, if you want to bludge or you don't want to do it just get out of our fucking way 'cos we're coming through.

That was the whole site mentality. No one gave a shit about anything because they were in a hurry to get the job done, and if the company didn't make any money, neither would they. It was a whole different culture and I took my hat off to them.

Middle management continued to plague us and to make life as difficult as they could, always looking for something we might have missed or asking for more paperwork. Every week something would change or they'd move something around and we were getting dragged over the coals the whole time we were there.

At the end of twelve months they gave us an opportunity to do some more work, but they were screwing us, wanting us to do a heap of non-funded stuff. At the end of it, I thought *nah, I'm not interested.* They were also playing us off against other

RTOs, whereas, originally, they'd never even heard about the system.

I just said, 'You guys should go with those other RTOs and rip someone else off for a while. We've given it a hundred percent for the past twelve months and no-one is going to give you what we have. We'll let you come back to us.' I do believe they would have, but the backside fell out of the whole gas industry and they ended up putting off about a thousand people. When it picks up again we'll be the guys back out there. We gave them a fantastic service, so they'd be silly not to take us on again. Middle-management wouldn't care, but the guys upstairs, the directors, they'd be a loyal bunch of guys. We committed to the job and we saw it through, I was very proud of that.

One last thing, out of the three hundred apprentices we were supposed to get, we ended up getting one hundred and twenty. They chose not to give us the rest of the guys on site. For one reason or another, they decided not to train them all, so we didn't really make any money out there either. We broke about even on the job.

However, we got a lot of industry recognition for it and we got a lot of work from other companies out there. RTOs had been trying to crack into Murphy Pipe and Civil for some time and getting nowhere because they couldn't get past middle management. The fact was that we got around them by doing our presentation to the directors and no one could work out how we'd scored the job at the time but it got us the kudos.

In fact, we got the job through Brendan, a guy up north. My cousin, Rob, was working on a mine up there which Murphy Pipe and Civil were on and I'd been speaking to him to get us on site. When Brendan moved to Wandala, Rob put me in touch with him. He was the superintendent on site, so he's not necessarily anyone too big. The buck doesn't stop with him; over him you've got the site engineer and then the site construction manager. But he was Irish and he knew the Murphy side of it and the directors, so he was able to give us the opportunity because all the directors were getting together for some major decision making in the head office. He was a hard customer. He liked what I offered and he gave me a lot of pointers on things to improve.

At first, his accent was so strong I couldn't understand a thing he was saying. I'm just nodding saying, 'Yes mate, uh huh, yep, yep.' And then he stopped talking and just looked at me while I'm nodding away. 'I asked a fucking question,' he said, glaring at me.

'Oh,' I stammered, 'I can't understand anything.' He'd well and truly caught me out.

He didn't want to give us this opportunity to present to the board of directors and for us to go in there unprepared and look like dickheads. So he gave us a list of things for us to do to make it work, and if we were prepared to do those things he'd be happy to set up the meeting. Of course we did, and he did.

I've already said how terrifying it was to walk into a room of nine directors from a billion-dollar company having never even spoken to anyone at that level. It was daunting because we didn't know what to expect. We were in there for five minutes and it only took that long to work out that these guys were no different to us. We're all pretty much equal in some way and they were just a bunch of Irish guys having a laugh.

The middle management guy, Stuart Cairns, who looked after training was away on holiday for a week while Brendan, the superintendent, had flown in to Brisbane for that meeting. When we finished the presentation we asked the chairman, Tom Dermody, what he thought. 'It sounds good,' he said.

'We'll have a talk with Stuart when he gets back from holiday and see what he thinks.'

Every RTO in the state knows that Stuart never returns emails, never returns phone calls, nothing. No one in the industry can make headway with him. So Brendan stood up and said, 'Tom, that's fine, we should get Stuart to sign off on this, but my problem is that I need these guys on site on Monday. Today's Friday, that only gives them the weekend to get organised and have them in on Monday. Could we give them some sort of green light so they can get going on a little bit of stuff then run it past Stuart?'

It was fortuitous that Stuart wasn't there because if he was he would have fought it. That's why he was so pissed off with us for the rest of the time. Everyone at the table looked down towards Tom and Tom said, in his best Irish accent, 'Oh fuck it, I'll smooth it over with him later.' Everybody laughed and off we went. It was crazy. And we didn't realise at the time how much Stuart would take umbrage. We had no way of knowing what we were in for.

Face-to-face

When I left the site and moved back to Brisbane, I had a little five metre by ten metre office on the main road of Strathpine. It was a tiny little thing and it cost me one hundred and fifty dollars a week.

I set up the shelving for the resources, bought a cheap printer to churn out all our own paperwork to get us started, and looked around for some sales guys to get out there and start talking to some companies. I was starting from scratch and building the same type of company up that I'd started up with John. Initially, I employed a few sales guys who were absolutely terrible. They were fantastic guys, but we just weren't getting anywhere and I was out there doing all the sales myself. At this point Paul Cameron pops back into my story.

For the past two years I'd kept in contact with him and, by then, his wife had left him and he was back working for a fencing company for a thousand dollars a week. He had the kids who he had to drop off and pick up from school so he could only work between those hours, and he simply wasn't making enough money to make ends meet. I pleaded with him to come and work for me as a sales guy and he kept telling me he wasn't a sales guy; he'd never done sales in his life. 'Paul,' I said. 'All you've ever done in your life is sales, that's all you are, you go around selling snake oil.'

'Thanks Paul,' he told me. 'But it's not for me.'

So we struggled along and did a few sign ups, and then finally, finally, I got Paul to come along and listen to what I had to tell him. This is when Face-to-Face really started to take off. Paul's exactly like me. He can do sales the way I do because I have no trouble going and knocking on someone's door and having a conversation with them. To me it's not sales, it's just the truth well told. Pauly was able to do the same thing. So now I've got myself a sales guy who's getting sales. On Pauly's first month he got a hundred enrolments for me. At that stage it was a million dollars' worth of work.

Over the first few months I'd made a few hundred sign-ups myself, so things were really starting to take off for us. Now with five salesmen I really started learning what sales are all about. Until then, I'd only just done it. It happened and I had no idea what we were doing or what we were not doing.

Now, knowing about sales is the most powerful thing for any sales company or any company at all out there wanting to sell. And every company needs to do sales, they just don't realise how big the need is. Here I am with these five sales guys and only one of them is doing any good. Paul can bring me a hundred enrolments a month and the other guys are bringing me about five enrolments a month each. I've had the other guys for about three months now and I've had Paul Cameron for one month and he can bring in one hundred enrolments but, the strange thing is, I liked the other guys more. The other guys are better to talk to, they come across as being more genuine to me, although that's mainly because I've known Paul Cameron for a long time and I know what he's like.

For the life of me I couldn't understand why I've got this one guy that can do all these sales and all these other guys can't. What is it that they're doing? What is it that they're not doing? What's happening? I'm thinking about this and trying to work out why and trying lots of different things, trying to motivate them and trying to work out where we're going or asking myself are they even working at all?

In this search for answers I went to a one-night training session with Jordan Belfort. It was then I realised what was going on in our organisation. Put simply, 'the hardest enemy to kill is the one you can't see.' When you can't see the problem you don't know how to solve it and I'd say ninety percent of the people in sales can't see the problem, they don't actually know what's going on, or what's going wrong. You don't know what you don't know.

Going to this one night with Jordan, I found that it's all the little things, things like tonality. When we're telling someone a secret we lower our voices, if we tell a story and we're very confident. We are loud and very direct about it. A big thing for Jordan is 'fair enough', he'd ask, 'Sound fair enough?' at the end of a sales pitch. Essentially what he's saying just with his tone and choice of words is, 'I'm a fair guy, you're a fair guy, this is a fair thing that we're looking at.' It's the tonality, it's the body language, it's the eye contact, it's everything that a person does from the start of the talk to the end of the talk. And the biggest thing — the ability to build rapport with a person straight away.

There is only five percent of the population that naturally have that sales ability. I, obviously, have it, Paul has it, and all the other guys, the ones I like more, don't have it. That five percent who do, don't even know what it is they do, they just do it. The most powerful thing that any sales trainer, sales manager, or company that has sales guys working for them, the most powerful thing you can work out, is what that guy is doing that those guys aren't. There's actually no magic in it, it's just science.

There are probably about ten things you can train those guys to do and, suddenly, they'll all become high achievers. That's what Jordan's movie is essentially about, the ability to train people to influence others. He's one of that five percent himself. He was able to work it out for himself, identify what he was doing that the other guys weren't, and then train them to do what he *was* doing.

That's the secret to his success and that's all he has. That's where Jordan makes his money; training people how to make money, and how they make money is by simply influencing people, simply becoming influencers. As evil as that may sound, listen, our kids influence us when they ask us to take them to the lolly shop or when they talk us into buying them a toy, 'But remember daddy you said you'd get me one last week,' and you think, *Oh man, did I?* 'Okay buddy let's go.' That's a prime example of how we're born knowing the art of persuasion, it's just that some people are better at it than others along with the ability to talk to people and the ability to build rapport with others. No one's going to buy a car off a person they feel no rapport with, they'll go down the road and still buy the same car at the same price, but they'll buy it from the guy they feel a rapport with. Those five sales guys that I had would go off and explain the course and the funding that was available and everything else about it, but a lot of the people they'd talk to would go and call another RTO and sign up with them. That says it all, the product is good and the case is airtight, they just don't like the guy that's trying to sell it.

The other huge thing is believing in whatever it is you're selling. If you can't show anyone that you believe in it, how do you expect them to believe in it? Jordan, Paul and I all have the ability to show our belief in what we're talking about. A lot of these little milestones were reached and our sales team started to snowball, to grow exponentially.

I'd seen Jordan's course advertised on a billboard. The funny thing is that I'd been over to Redcliffe to have a meeting with somebody, and this was the area where I worked for John. There I am driving back home on the Hornibrook Highway at seven in the morning and the seminar was in three days' time. It was a one-day event and a preview to selling his boot camp. It cost seven hundred dollars a ticket and I bought two tickets. Well, it was actually three hundred dollars a ticket and for seven hundred dollars you could go back to the after party and get your book signed.

I didn't give a stuff about the signing but I wanted to meet the guy and understand it all, so I paid the fourteen hundred dollars to go to the after party and he was sitting in a chair silent and completely shattered. As I've discovered, public speaking is very draining, standing in a room full of people giving it your all for hours on end, you've not got much left. So, the money was not well spent because no one got to talk to him. There would have been about a thousand people there and about twenty went to the after party. Of course I signed up for the boot camp, taking five of us down to Melbourne, paying thirty thousand for all of us to attend the course. And, for Face-to-Face, and me, it was the beginning of a wild roller coaster ride.

LEARNING THE GAME

The things we learnt at Jordan's boot camp, or even things I learnt that first night in Brisbane at Jordan's 'pull the suckers into the boot camp' talk, changed our whole business.

The number one thing is building rapport with people. If you build rapport with someone they simply want to be with you, there are no two ways about that. But if you don't have a rapport with someone and you haven't made it all about being in rapport them, even though you've given them an airtight case to buy, they'll want that product and they will still buy it. They just won't buy it off you.

That was the case for us, we probably lost a lot of students simply because our guys didn't strike up a good rapport with them. There's a lot more to understanding what rapport is and building it up than meets the eye. If a sales guy walks into someone's office and sees they've got a fish up on the wall, they'll start talking about fishing and think they've struck up a rapport. But they could be coming across as a wanker and unprofessional.

Rapport is coming across as being a professional and proving yourself to be one, at the same time being a likeable and understanding sort of person. It's good to have similar

PAUL CONQUEST

interests but not when it's a contrived attempt to establish rapport.

Rapport is the number one sales tool, and there are many ways to be in rapport with a lot of training that goes into that. It's more than just giving someone the do's and don'ts.

There are many ways to stay in rapport, and the first is tonality. You can control a whole conversation with tonality, you can show that you believe in whatever you may be talking about, you can add scarcity into the conversation by using tonality, and you can add authority, likability and empathy. It all depends on the way it's used.

Training someone to use the tone of their voice effectively can change sales overnight. Combine it with body language and it's a hit. People need to be trained not to let their body language become louder than their words. Strange as it sounds, it's a very common mistake.

For example, if I'm talking to someone biting their nails, I'm instantly out of rapport with that person. I read them as a nervous type who may not be too certain of what they're talking about, and doesn't come across as professional. The way I shake someone's hand, the importance of not being in someone's face, looking someone in the eyes, they are all so important. Tonality and body language builds rapport. Interestingly, in the past, Jordan got himself into trouble with his ability to get people into deep rapport, because they then tended to do whatever he wanted them to do.

So those are the two biggest things in sales. Another important one is learning how to ask for a referral correctly. If I'm a great sales guy with a fantastic product, ninety percent of my sales will come from referrals rather than being out there hunting and gathering. The average salesperson fails to become great because they miss referrals.

Here in Australia, we all want to help each other, therefore the word 'help' can be used effectively in a couple of ways: 'Do you know anyone else we could help with this product?' Or, 'This is great, it's a great product and a great fit for you, is there any way you can help me and maybe give me anyone else that could benefit from what we're doing here today?' The art of asking for a referral is very powerful. Done right it doubles business right there and then.

On top of all that, we needed an effective script. Everyone says something a little differently, so guys who are working really well and getting lots of sales will have different language patterns. But there will be one best way, so if everyone works off the same script, saying the same thing and giving the same information, it will double sales.

As much as a script can sound wooden, and sales guys don't generally like to work off a script because they fear they'll sound like a salesman, if they practice that script over and over and get it right, it's like being a good actor. An actor is working off a script but has to practice it, otherwise it's obvious and the movie's going to be crap. A comedian is working off a script. Comedians aren't necessarily funny people, but when they're working on stage they need to work off the script that's been written so that they come across as funny on stage. And they just need to be funny when they're in front of an audience, and that brings me to the next thing — emotional state.

A person's emotional state is manageable. If a sales guy finds the right emotional state when they're talking about something, they come across as confident, certain and knowledgeable. A salesperson can't expect someone to believe what they themselves don't appear to believe in.

The elements that made a good or poor salesperson were made clear to me that first night. It was there, right in front of me. As I've said, the hardest enemy to kill is the one you can't see, and it's not until you realise what's making the difference between the great salesperson and the not-so-great salesperson that you can then turn all your people into great salespeople. Of course, turning everyone into awesome salespeople came right around and eventually bit me in the bum. Actually, it took a huge fucking chunk out of it.

In no time, we had an unstoppable army of truly excellent salespeople. We grew fast, really fast. Then we attracted attention — lots of it. Clearly we were doing the wrong thing. The industry couldn't appreciate that our enormous success could be by doing things right. The fact is, we were, and then Jordan came on board and it went ballistic.

~

Everyone in sales understands that if it's too good to be true, it probably is. However, in the training industry, it definitely sounds too good to be true, but it actually is true. The qualifications cost the employer virtually nothing — in fact, there's cash back for them. The trainer goes out on site, the off-work time is minimised, and the employee gets something really worthwhile. What a marvellous product. Why would anyone need a salesperson for it?

Many RTOs are struggling and that didn't make sense to me. What I've learnt since is that ten percent of people are what is called a 'laydown sale', so they're the easy people to sell to — the low hanging fruit. The other ninety percent of the market are not in that category. They have to be worked for a sale, regardless of the fact it's being given away.

Because the training industry is so lucrative, the majority of RTOs are living off that ten percent and making good money off it. We didn't do that. We weren't interested in just the ten percent, we wanted the other ninety percent, and I wanted to learn how to get to it.

To do that, I learnt about 'front loading'. If a sale is front loaded, all the benefits are presented right at the start. It doesn't matter how valuable the product is or what the benefits are, it sounds like a cosmetic dental ad. And that's talking the prospect out of a sale.

Anyone new to the sales industry who jumps in and gives the prospect of all the benefits will only get that ten percent. The other ninety percent is captured by writing a more informative script. I say, 'Don't tell them everything that's in it for them, let them know what we do and give them a little bit of information. Script it out a little bit more accurately, and then slowly roll out the benefits during the conversation. Build rapport and then introduce the benefits.' There's obviously a lot more to it.

After learning those new sales tools we saw huge results in the first week back after the boot camp. For me, being one of the five percent of natural salesmen, I learnt a lot. I understood what I was doing that worked and was able to polish it. It almost doubled my own sales. It well over doubled the sales rate for others who didn't have those skills to begin with. And the learning never ends, for myself or anybody. The learning and the journey of learning never ends, the learning of new skills plus new ways to strengthen those skills.

The boot camp in Melbourne was about two months after Jordan's preview and took place over three days. I didn't take the whole sales team; I only took five of us. One was the company's general manager (Johnny Mac), others were, Rob Ford (my cousin), Paul Cameron, and another salesperson.

The only ones who really bought into the course were myself, Paul and the other salesperson. Early on, I could see that Rob and Johnny weren't getting anything out of it. They took no notes and weren't excited at all, whereas I'd be jumping out of my skin at the end of each day. Their response was, 'Oh yeah, when you've been to one of these things you've been to them all haven't you? They're all the same, I can't wait to get back to Brisbane. I'm over it.'

Even now, it's the same. You've still got to find the ones who want to learn and understand it all. If they don't understand it, or don't want to understand it, it's not going to do them any good. It has to excite.

We went back to Brisbane with our newfound knowledge, trained the other three sales people, and put the polish on Paul. Then I implemented a sales training programme where I'd get the sales team in at five every morning. They absolutely hated that. My attitude was, 'If you don't like it there are plenty of other places you can work for, but good luck with that and there will be plenty of other people who would like to work here.'

So they'd come in at five so they could be out to work at six. Their argument was, why can't we do the training over the phone or on Skype, or whatever? I explained that it was a lot more powerful in person and, in fact, if I had them there between 5 and 6am and sending them out at six, I knew they were actually out of bed and on their way out to site, because we're in the construction industry, and a lot of construction starts at six.

Bringing them in early was motivationally important, and getting them into that certain state set them up for the day. It was a very different thing to rolling out of bed and wandering onto site each day. Bringing them in each morning, getting them into that certain state, getting them excited about the day and what they were going to do, and giving them some ideas of what to do. Which sites they could visit, work on their marketing, and so on.

The only thing we were doing differently to other RTOs was training our sales people a lot better and a lot more efficiently. We trained them how to profile people, using a personality profile assessment tool. We'd use it on each other to become familiar and confident with the DiSC profiler. DiSC stands for the personality types: Dominance, Influence, Steadiness and Conscientiousness. It's a powerful, accurate fifteen-minute test, and very useful. I mentioned it briefly talking about John.

I'm a D-I with a high D, along with five percent of the population. This means I'm highly driven, and you find a lot of these people are CEOs, directors of companies and so on. The dark side of the D type is that they are bullies, so they tend to talk over others, they tend to think that what they have to say is more important than what others have to say. That's what we do, we're bullies and we tend to get angry and that's typical of me. I can say, 'Mate I just don't care about your opinion, just do what I asked you to do.' I'm a classic, raving, high D.

In sales, you learn how to curb that so you don't upset others. The best way to deal with a bullying high D is to stand up to them. You don't get into a fight with them, but you don't back down, and the way to not back down is to give them facts and figures. I can guarantee that if anyone ever brings facts and figures to me, they'll beat me every time, because that's all I want from people. Just give me a snapshot, just give me the facts and figures and let's move on. And that's easy to do in sales, give the facts and figures.

A high C is a high compliance person, they're commonly accountants and lawyers and they're great doing that. The thing with the high C is that they want to know more about what you're talking about than you know. So, if you're doing a presentation to a high C, they'll ask you to leave a bit of information with them and they'll get you to come back in a day or two. By the time you get back, they'll want to prove you wrong. The downside of a high C can be a 'holier than thou,' attitude. What you never, ever do with a high C is prove them wrong. If you ever prove them to be wrong, you've blown the sale right there and then, and you've probably blown the friendship. You might have won the argument, but they're just going to walk off.

In a training session, or a course, when the guy up the front is asking and someone gives a wrong answer, they'll say something like, 'Yep, yep, anyone else have any thoughts?' Until they get to the answer they want, they're not going to say, 'No you're wrong,' because they don't know what personality type the people are and therefore don't want to lose rapport with the room. If I'm selling to a high C and they say something that's inaccurate, I don't point it out to them, I just say, 'Yes there's that, and here's another way you could do it.'

About twenty percent of the population is high I — a high influencing person. They are great at talking to people, they're great with different personalities and at explaining things to them. They can influence people to do things their way. The negative thing with the high I is that they're very selfish. I'm not saying they'll put themselves over other people, but I can be talking to an I and they can ask you how your weekend went and you can say, 'Oh yeah, I went to the beach and...' and then they'll jump in and say, 'Oh awesome! I went to the beach as well, and I did this and I did that...' They like to talk about themselves more than they like to talk about others. So, the one thing I need to know about the high I is to make the conversation about them, don't make it about myself. They can talk to me all day, as long as I can slip in what it is I want to talk about.

Sixty-five percent of the population has a high S personality profile. The high S is very steady, very reliable, the kind of person that may work for the same company or person for ten or twenty years. They're not out trying to change the world, they're just there trying to do their bit, and do their bit for society. They're caring people and very trustworthy.

The problem with the high S is that, although they are trustworthy, they are very distrustful and suspicious, so it's a bit harder to build trust with them than a high D. A salesperson may give me a good spiel about what they're selling and I'll probably buy two or three of them. A high S would not. That person first needs to build trust and rapport before anything else, and with them it probably takes a couple more touch points. I might want to make a phone call and follow it up with an email and then pop out and see them before I can start to build that relationship. The great thing about that is that once I do build that trust with the high S, I've found myself a customer for life because they're steady, reliable and loyal.

The downfall of the high S is that they're compulsive liars. My wife is a raving high S. She's the highest high S I've ever known. I'm not saying she cheats with the neighbour and lies to me about it, or anything like that, but if I said, 'Do you think my gut's getting big?' she'd say, 'No, of course not, you look great Paul.' If she gets a sales call she'll say, 'That sounds great, but I'm busy right now, can I call you back later?' and she's never going to call back. She's lying. The high S person will compulsively lie just to get out of confrontations. They dislike confrontation immensely. My wife can't stand confrontation. If we're buying a car and I'm haggling with the car salesman, she has to walk away. She can't even handle that little bit of confrontation, even being around someone who's having a small confrontation, so she's the high end of that spectrum. Talking to them, most high Ss will say, 'Call me back,' or 'I'll call you back next week,' they're just trying to get away. Me, as a high D, would say to the salesman, 'Mate that sounds shit, don't ever call me again.' You would never have to wonder what I might be thinking, but a high S wouldn't do that. That is powerful knowledge to a sales person.

Now, everyone has a 'native tongue,' but we can change who we are, everything about ourselves if we want to. However, it's no different than an Italian coming to Australia, living here for ten years, and speaking fluent English. If the Italian becomes angry, upset, or distressed, they'll go back to their native tongue and start shouting in Italian.

I can change who I am in a sale, or be in a certain emotional state. I can be whoever I need to be, and control who I am, but when someone upsets me or sets me off, I'll find myself speaking over them, and I will have reverted back to my natural persona. I can control it to an extent, but the fact that I can understand what I've done wrong because I understand my personality profile well means I can walk away and think about it. I can then go back and apologise. Yes, I do quite a bit of apologising. I try to control myself, try to understand myself, but everyone has a native tongue and, like everyone else, I often go back to mine. It's a little bit like the Incredible Hulk; he knows he's done the wrong thing, and he just has to go back and apologise afterwards.

Obviously, the S types were the people that we were particularly interested in. We learned how to build rapport and trust with them, to get those people that other companies couldn't get. If I turn up in front of an S and front load, that is spray out all the advantages and benefits, they're just not going to trust me. They'll just ask me to leave a bit of information with them and say they'll get back to me. Of course they never will.

I find that part of sales particularly fascinating because it's like going fishing. There are different types of hooks, baits and lines, and each of these work on different types of fish at different times of the day. Looking at this as an analogy of work, I'm excited to go every day. We'll try a little bit of this, we'll try a little bit of that, and we'll keep on fine tuning it until we become professional fishermen.

At our three-day induction with new sales people, one of the first things we do is a DiSC test. We explain where everybody fits in and we'll make them write whatever they are and put that on the desk in front of them. This is the best way to get them to understand not only their traits but the traits of everyone else. If someone starts talking over someone else, everyone has a laugh and says, 'Ah, look at that high D guy over there,' or if someone comes in and starts talking about themselves they'd think, 'Hmm, there's a high I.'

We also train our staff in the four levels of learning. The first stage is *You Don't Know What You Don't Know* and, for that, we use a baby as an analogy. A baby knows nothing, yet doesn't understand that they don't know anything. This level is called Unconsciously Incompetent.

The second stage of learning is *Consciously Incompetent*. Just like a child in the back seat of a car, they know that it takes skill to drive a car, but they don't have that skill yet. What we're doing in the first day of training is showing them the skills and what they can do with these skills, making them consciously incompetent; knowing what it is they don't know.

They then become *Consciously Competent*. This is when they're shown the skills, just like when a seventeen-year-old first learns how to drive a car. They can drive it but they have to think about what they're doing, they have to think about letting the clutch out, think about the accelerator and so on. They're now able to drive that car but it's a bit jerky, it's getting from A to B, and they have to think about it every step of the way. They're now consciously competent.

When they're *Unconsciously Competent*, they're at the place I am. Because they're so competent, they can drive around for hours and not even think about it. That's where we like to get our people with our DiSC test. If we can get our people to become unconsciously competent at reading people's personality profiles, and to profile someone very quickly and easily, that can dramatically improve sales. Being able to unconsciously read people wherever they go and whoever they see, makes that person a master at sales. It can be very easy to get people to those levels just by playing fun games around the office and by having everyone consistently profiling each other and having a friendly laugh at people's personality traits. If it's done correctly, a newcomer can become an unconsciously competent salesperson in about three months.

Last year, just before everything went pear-shaped I was setting up a sales qualification because it's remarkable how few people know this stuff in Australia. Some people know bits of it, others know other parts, but no one knows it all. To bring all that together as a package changes a sales guy's life very, very quickly. When they understand themselves and understand others, understand why people make decisions the way they do, and say the things that they say, it's essentially science and no longer sales. That's what got Jordan into so much trouble, his ability to understand and read people so well.

We did all this before Jordan came along. We went to his boot camp but we were using the DiSC test long before that. After the boot camp I went back to Brisbane and started researching and reading up on sales training, doubling the information and skills I'd brought away from the three days with Jordan.

Apart from the reading, I had a sales colleague, Wade Grundon, come on board with us for a while. Wade was an ex-business coach, so a lot of good stuff came from him. I had an instant feeling about Wade. He's a short, unassuming sort of guy and I'd done work for him in the past when he was the manager of another company.

The company he was with had gone into administration. It was closing down and he was looking for somewhere to go. I went and had a chat with him, unaware at that stage that he used to be a business coach going around coaching other businesses. On his first day on the job with us, everyone was struck by how engaging he was. We couldn't help but love the guy. He didn't know any of the stuff that I was rolling out, and I didn't know any of the stuff that he was rolling out, so we more or less put everything together and moved forward from there.

With us for about eighteen months, Wade didn't like it when Jordan came on board because Jordan took the spotlight from that point onwards. They clashed and Jordan was critical of Wade, and I believe Jordan was harsh on him. Wade took Jordan's criticisms to heart and shrank, stopped being the vibrant lively guy that he'd been, allowing himself to be crushed, and was essentially left by the wayside. How did that happen?

To inspire others, you first have to be inspired yourself. For example, if anyone was to do some public speaking and wanted to know how to inspire a room, something very tough when it's day in and day out, I'd tell them that they had to be inspired themselves. There's no other way. If you can show that you're inspired, you believe in what you are talking about, and you're one hundred percent, that will come through in your tonality, body language and everything that you have to offer.

I guess when Jordan came on board it was hard for Wade to be inspired because he wasn't 'that guy' anymore. Jordan was 'that guy'. It's funny how inspiration can suddenly switch off.

Recently, post-Jordan, coming up with a new business model and wanting to get started, I got Wade back again. I asked him if he wanted to be part of it and he did, but he was flat. He had so much head trash because of his history with Jordan. Two weeks into the job, he decided that the job wasn't working for him and he resigned. Jordan actually liked him and said he was a great guy, but Wade let himself become diminished when Jordan became the number one guy, and consequently lost his wonderful inspirational quality.

DRIVING FORCES

The difference between a successful and unsuccessful person is that a successful person is not scared of failure. They're not scared to continue to fail because they know, sooner or later, they're going to succeed.

When a project fails, I believe a person goes through a series of emotions, but, on me, they don't weigh very heavily. It doesn't discourage me from moving forward. I might get a bit annoyed about what might have been for a while, but at the same time I see a failure not as failing but as an opportunity to learn.

It actually stimulates me, so what happened with Face-to-Face training was exciting. It was another chapter in my life that gave me the opportunity to learn from my mistakes, and I know the next chapter is going to be better.

It's electrifying knowing that whatever you're going to be doing in the future will be with new lessons learnt. It's not about money either. The more money I make, the more I realise that it's not about that. Since I was twenty, I've always had the philosophy of not caring when I lose money. I can always get more. Really.

Money's just a product of my success. My lifestyle doesn't change whether I've got a lot of money or no money. Not much changes because it's all the little things that I enjoy in life like my family, the ability to wake up and have breakfast in the morning with them, all those things that I love, and I can't change that. No matter how hard things get, I can't imagine not being able to put food on the table, I can't believe that I couldn't go out and get a job. I've never been unemployed, ever, and I can't imagine being so, or being in a position where I couldn't add value to someone somewhere.

When we went to the boot camp, I thought Jordan was an extremely smart guy, but he didn't have the time to talk to anyone in particular, so there was no opportunity to have a lengthy conversation, or have an opportunity to warm to him.

I guess I was a bit in awe of him, and it's a little embarrassing to say that. Mainly, he had all the answers to all the questions that I'd been looking for. Suddenly, it all made sense to me and everything became clear. That's the reason I bought into it one hundred percent. I just loved the guy and wanted to get to know him better.

He's an interesting guy. He's lived an interesting life and he's like two different people. When he's on stage or with a group of people, I think he feels the need to entertain everyone and be charismatic. But, when he's by himself, he's rather shy and quiet. In fact, he's very much like me.

We used to have a dinner party at his place once a week. Each time, he'd come up with a new story to tell, and the whole table would be enthralled. He'd get lots of laughs, but straight after that, after dinner and a couple of drinks, you could see he'd just want to get out of there and go to bed. You could see him hit a wall, because when he became that person, putting himself in that state, it's very, very draining. It sucks the energy out.

It's no different when he's on stage. He's so energetic and charismatic because that's what he does, and that's what he trains other people to do. The person on stage is far from the person he really is, which would be the same for most actors, I'd imagine. I've heard that Robert De Niro is a really quiet, shy guy.

When I do a presentation, it's exactly the same. At the end of it I'm exhausted. Last week I was starting some new sales drives and interviewed three guys back-to-back. When I want the best guys to come and work for me, I still have to sell myself to them. So, after interviewing three guys one after the other I was shattered, because I'm explaining everything to them, I'm making it sound exciting, I'm using the right tonalities, enthusiasm, body language — everything. It's no different talking to one person than it is talking to three, or four, or even a stadium full.

CRACKS IN THE FOUNDATIONS

When we began the process of purchasing Face-to-Face, there was already a part-time compliance manager there; Wendy Owen. I could see that as we were gaining students and momentum so quickly, we needed a compliance manager full-time and Wendy agreed to do it.

Everything with ASQA, the federal regulator, and the state regulators, required that we do everything correctly and abide by their rules. The compliance manager oversees this, as well as ensuring the students are being looked after correctly and are happy, making sure that there's a watchdog for the trainers, putting systems in place, looking at the checkpoints, and making sure the trainers are doing the correct amount of training.

A CEO of a company can do it himself. It really depends on the size of the company, how fast it grows, or how big it wants to be. At that stage we didn't really need a compliance manager. I could have managed it. However, I didn't know the industry well enough and I had concerns that, if I missed anything, it could be detrimental to the whole company and it's goals.

We were being more compliant than we needed to be and I was happy with that. In my opening talk with Wendy, I assured her that she had my full backing for anything she wanted to do, and this had to be taken more seriously than anything else. I knew that the one thing that was going to keep the company going was being compliant in the industry, and had to be taken more seriously than anything else.

The entire company was made aware that compliance ran the company. They were making the rules and we all had to abide by them. That's how the company was always going to be run, and it's how it always was run. Wendy was also told that she had an open cheque book for compliance.

When a trainer goes out and trains someone and the paperwork comes back, most RTOs across the industry check ten percent of it. We checked absolutely everything that came back. We had a validator that checked every piece of paper to make sure that everything had been filled in correctly, that all the signatures were right, and that everything had been dated. We had to make sure that we'd got the students' signatures to prove that they were happy with the outcome of their training.

We were paid very well for what we were doing, and I wanted to let everybody know that we were going to give a great product in return. I think the secret to a successful company is giving value for money, so if you're going to get paid very well, you've got to give great value. For us, that was what it was all about; giving great value to our students and trying to find a way that we could grow while keeping everything compliant, putting all the systems required in place to make sure we stayed compliant.

By the end of it, Wendy had a compliance team of approximately thirty people. In the beginning, there was just herself and one validator who would look through all the paperwork to make sure it was correct. So compliance and value to students were our two biggest priorities. We grew very

THE TRUTH WELL TOLD

quickly, but compliance was always fine, and all the checks and balances were done.

The biggest problem, and something we missed, was that suddenly Jordan was in the company and he's motivating sales guys to go out and sign people up. That's where we fell over a bit, and this is how it came about.

Right at the start, there was something else compliance-wise we did and were heavily invested in. As I've said, we'd bring our sales guys in every morning for an hour and train them on what to say, what they're allowed to say, and what they're not allowed to say. As a result, everyone in the company clearly knew the type of student that suited our business model, and to make sure they didn't sign up anyone not falling into that criteria.

Jordan wasn't as clear on that and didn't understand it well enough. Suddenly, we had a whole lot of sales guys who wanted to come and work for us, keen to be trained by Jordan. But the quality of their enrolments wasn't as good, resulting in the higher possibility of buyers' remorse (when someone signs up for a course and then changes their mind when they realise it isn't quite the right fit for them). That's fine, but then the sales guys get upset thinking that it's the company who has scuppered the sale. Remember that sales people were only paid after the person they'd signed up was trained.

We never had that problem in the early days because I was very thorough on whom we signed up. The other problem was that a trainer would often go out to see a student and, on the first visit, immediately see that the student was simply not the right person for the course. It could be a pregnant woman with six children, and they've signed her in for a Cert III in driving operations. We'd say, 'That woman is never going to drive a truck, what is wrong with you guys? She's eligible, if she wants to do it, but she's doing it for the wrong reasons.' To control that, we'd cancel those enrolments. Again, the guy that enrolled them gets upset because his enrolments haven't gone through and he's not going to get paid for them. So, by growing so fast, small fires started up around the place. And that's how we got into trouble with the media.

When we sacked some of our less-conscientious sales people, they went to the media and complained about not getting paid. They claimed that we weren't visiting our students and had conflicts with all of them. This was simply not true. We had rules around everything that we did, we were following them, and had a paper trail to prove it.

~

We began to see that, inadvertently, Jordan's training methods were flawed. For the first couple of weeks, he would come in himself to do the training. But then he sent some of his guys to do it for him — people he knew in Australia and had already worked with him.

Remember, I had a core sales team, guys who initially hated coming at five am for a sales meeting, but eventually came to love it. We all enjoyed each other's company, we'd put on some brekkie, talk about compliance and who they should talk to and general target markets, and we'd make it a bit of fun.

On the first day of Jordan's management team, we asked them to be there at five in the morning. They blew up, they wouldn't have it, they said it was ridiculous, it was unheard of, why would you possibly want to do that? I said, 'Guys, if you don't want to work here that's up to you, that's bad luck, but if you do want to work here you, those are the rules, you have to be here at five am.'

Jordan wasn't there at the time, but his team got him to give me a call to tell me that it was unreasonable. The argument went on for about a month before we agreed to meet in the middle. At that stage, I let go. I thought that maybe I was being a little bit unreasonable, maybe five o'clock doesn't work for everybody, maybe they were too tired. Those guys obviously knew more about sales than I did, so I'm going to have to take the back seat a little bit.

And I did take the back seat a little and let it run its course. I reasoned that maybe I had something to learn. And I absolutely did. If I had the time over again, I would have hung on to what we had and I would have continued doing what we had been doing.

We started to get a lot more enrolments. At the end of 2014 and the start of 2015, before Jordan came along, we had a saying with the sales team: 'We're going to do 2015 signups in one month sometime during 2015'. That was our goal. After Jordan arrived, at the end of 2015, we were doing four thousand enrolments a month. At the beginning of 2015, two thousand enrolments were unheard of, it just wasn't imagined, it seemed like a ridiculous number.

To put it into perspective, back then, we were probably doing one hundred and fifty enrolments a week, so about six hundred a month. We went from six hundred a month to four thousand a month in quite a short time. As much as the sales grew, we still weren't really trying. We were holding the sales people back because it was a struggle training all the students efficiently.

We had to get out and train all those guys so, at that point, I had to put on a full-time training manager to manage the trainers. I also put on five full-time mentors to mentor the trainers, to make sure everyone was getting the support they needed to train the students. And we put on a full-time trainer to train us how to be better trainers. This person was taken from the industry to support the growth that was taking place with all the new students.

We were trying to hold the sales guys back a bit at this point. We weren't motivating them, we were trying to give ourselves time to get on top of the whole training side of the business. I was feeling pretty nervous about things at that time, and when Jordan and his team started I was really concerned because I knew we had a pile of sales guys out there that weren't trained the way we were insisting that they should be trained.

Right from the beginning, Jordan brought in about twenty new sales people, so the team went from ten to thirty overnight. That was huge. He also brought in Leigh Storr, someone he'd worked with in the past. As soon as Jordan decided that he wanted to come on board with us, he rang Leigh in Melbourne, showed him our business plan and said, 'This is a great company Leigh, and it's a great idea. Are you in or out? You have to tell me now. If you're in, you have to start tomorrow.'

Leigh was there the next day. He's been in the solar industry, had taken a company from zero to fifty million in its first twelve months and was nominated for Entrepreneur of the Year in Queensland. That's when he went to Jordan for advice and got to know him.

Leigh turned out to be a pain in the arse. He's a great guy but he's not practical. I believe he's got Asperger's — he's a genius, but everything is black and white to him, and there are no grey areas. I had to deal with this guy, talk to him, work with him, and he's dobbing me in to Jordan about what I will or won't allow him to do and so on. So there was a lot of politics going on and the whole company changed its dynamics overnight.

I first had the idea of inviting Jordan on board when I was still somewhat in awe of him. It didn't seem like a bad idea at the time. I thought I'd contact him, have a chat, and get him to do some training with our team. I was also aware that it could cause a bit of trouble within the industry but, at the same time, I thought, *we're not doing anything wrong, our compliance is over and above, we're doing everything right. We're not breaking any rules or laws so we've got nothing to worry about.* That's where my mind was; that he could help our company grow and we could be very successful. As much as he'd made his mistakes in the past, everything that he trained and taught at that point was about integrity and doing the right thing. There wasn't anything other than that and there never had been the whole time we were at the boot camp. He pushes integrity because of the name that he has, and there's really no other way for him.

I couldn't see what could possibly go wrong. If I could get Jordan to come and work with me personally, I was going to get all the best sales guys in the country wanting to come and work for me because it would show how much I'm investing in my guys and in my company. Also, what sort of RTO or company would we be if we weren't training our own guys, if we were out there telling everyone the importance of training and then not giving them the best possible training? And who better to do that than 'the best sales trainer on the planet', as he calls himself. It just made sense. As much as he's been branded a fraudster and a criminal, we weren't doing a single thing wrong. What's the worst that could happen? Obviously, I now know, but there's no way I could have seen it at the time.

ROTTEN TO THE CORE

Having experienced a four-week audit by DET, it's somewhat strange for me to say that DET and ASQA don't audit companies enough. I'll get to my delightful and woefully unsuccessful audit experience later but, for now, it's all about the training industry. There are many things being overlooked in it and a blatant practice of unfair targeting and favouritism.

I owned Face-to-Face for five years and never had an ASQA audit on our quality of training. The Courier-Mail even had a piece saying that ASQA had stated that they were considering revoking any qualification that Face-to-Face had given and making those people do it again.

I don't know how they can say such a thing when they've never even come and audited us against the quality of our training. Although we weren't being audited, we were actually paying someone to audit us privately because we wanted to remain compliant. And, because we hadn't been audited in five years, we knew it was only a matter of time, and when it happened we wanted to ace it. Because we were in it for the long haul, we wanted to be very compliant, but it never happened. We were closed down and then audited against licences — something previously unheard of. But I'm getting ahead of myself. Let me tell you a bit about the dodgy world of enrolments first.

To do an enrolment, we had to go out on site with someone from an apprenticeship centre, which is another company contracted by the state government to do the necessary paperwork required to activate the funding.

When someone says they want to do an apprenticeship, or a qualification, and we go onsite to do an enrolment with them, we would normally organise for the apprenticeship centre to be there at the same time. It's not necessary, but it makes good sense, thus saving the student and the employer time and not messing them around. Our whole system revolves around reducing disruption to a minimum in the workplace.

So, we'd meet the students and apprenticeship centre on site, run through our enrolment processes (about twenty minutes) and get the paperwork done. Easy when you're used to it.

My first day on the job was really scary for me. I had a room of ten guys and I had to do the enrolments myself. I wasn't totally on top of it, but I went ahead and did my bit. Now, there was a guy from an apprenticeship centre 'Busy at Work' present to do the sign-up on behalf of the government. That was Les Shaw. He was one hundred percent responsible for ensuring that the students were eligible for funding, not me. I was the training provider and there to make the training as user-friendly as possible. Busy at Work are paid by the government to oversee the eligibility criteria and the funding, and then they are paid to do site visits to make sure that the client is happy.

On the first day with Les, we went into the crib hut to sign up these guys, and he'd do his part first and explain everything, and then he asked everyone if they were full-time permanent. A few guys in the room said, 'no' because they were casual.

Being a full-time permanent is part of the eligibility criteria, so Les called me over and quietly told me that he couldn't sign anyone up that wasn't full-time permanent. He said that he might just step outside and have a smoke while I talk to them and then, when he comes back inside, he just wants them to say what he needs to hear.

Remember, this is my first ever enrolment and this guy is there representing the government. I had a bad feeling about what he was proposing, but I said, 'OK'. But, in the end, we didn't actually enrol those particular guys because I felt uncomfortable having to go back inside and have that conversation with them. I felt if they weren't eligible they weren't eligible. It was no big deal, there were plenty of guys out there who were eligible.

Moving along from that site, he told me about the next enrolment I had to do was a fencing company, one I happened to know very well at the time. He mentioned the same thing again, saying he'd rung the accounts person there, she had all the information, and she'd informed him that a lot of their guys were contractors, not all full-timers.

There were fifteen enrolments to do there, and a lot of those guys wouldn't be eligible for funding unless they said they were full-timers while Les was there. So I rang the company and told them what Les had said. Sure enough, when we got there everyone claimed to be full-time permanent employees. An amazing transformation.

Little did I know that the whole industry was doing it like that. Nor did I realise that the sales guys who were finding these people were also part of the system. Discovering that there were very few people around who would not sign someone up because they didn't hold the right employment status was a valuable lesson. At the end of the day, everyone had KPIs — key performance indicators, a type of performance measurement — that they had to meet and that's the way the whole industry is set up.

One of the biggest problems is that everyone gets paid per enrolment, or everybody's got a certain number of enrolments that they have to do. This flows all the way down from the state government. The whole system is set up to fail because an RTO gets paid ten thousand dollars per person as the paperwork goes through, so then an RTO would pay a trainer two thousand dollars per person to go out and find the person competent.

A trainer doesn't get paid to go out and find people not competent, they only get paid if they find people competent. How many people out there do you think would be found not yet competent when there's so much money riding on it? Not many. Shouldn't a trainer get paid to go out whether that person's competent or not? The sales guy gets paid per enrolment so, obviously, he's keen to get out there and do as much as he can. It's outcome-based, but the only way that can really work is if the RTOs are getting audited against what they're actually doing out there, and that's not happening.

We tried to do it our own way. We would bring someone in and audit our own systems regularly, which was very expensive. We would bring someone in for four thousand dollars a day two days a month and audit ourselves against ourselves. We'd have a compliance team and they were given the reigns to the whole company.

So as much as you can see what the dangers are there, and what's wrong with the industry, we really wanted to be compliant and sustainable. I wanted us to grow into a large education company, and I knew that couldn't happen without us remaining compliant.

Yes, we had people doing the wrong thing, but no company on the planet can honestly say they don't. It's whether a company is prepared to search for and stamp out those people that makes the difference. In a flawed industry, that's extremely difficult, it's challenging, and for me, incredibly exciting. OK, let's talk about me again then.

For me, being the CEO of a large company is a twenty-four hour a day job where I'm dealing with hundreds of small fires. I love it. But, it's not managing the day-to-day stuff that makes someone successful, we can all be trained to do that. It's foreseeing the problems of tomorrow, and it's understanding and learning from mistakes that spell success.

A person can't be trained to be successful in university. Experience and learning from mistakes don't come from study, they come from making mistakes again and again and again until the lessons are learnt.

It's practical, real world experience, focussing on things that may go wrong before they become problems, or turning those problems into potential opportunities that teaches us success. No progress is made in the comfort zone, that's the road to nowhere. If I'm not scared about something, or I don't have anxiety about something, then I'm probably not moving forward at all.

To be a successful business person doesn't mean knowing what I'm doing and just doing it. I step outside my comfort zone to learn new things. Not many people would believe that I'm a very quiet and shy person. I often have to put that aside and dig deep, find whoever I need to be at the time and get on with it. My biggest challenge? It's still, after all these years, speaking in front of people. I'm terrified of it.

THE RUNAWAY TRAIN

I've got Leigh on board and Jordan's flying in and out. Three weeks on, two weeks off, and on his two weeks off he's doing his speaking events all over the world.

When he initially came to do his speaking event for us, I was going to pay him one hundred and fifty thousand dollars for spending one day with us. Instead, we ended up paying three hundred thousand for spending two days. That was a staggering and frightening investment, but, after talking to Jordan on the phone, I knew it was the right thing to do.

We didn't have a lot of money at the time. Things were starting to go well but we were spending our money on resources, new training material, new systems, and getting with the future. The turnover was excellent, but we still living from month to month. Before Jordan came along, our turnover was something like seven or eight hundred thousand dollars. But we'd employed a huge number of compliance and validation staff, there was a large number of trainers, and everyone was getting paid very well because they were required to do, and did, a great job.

Jordan was already going to be in Australia for a three-day speaking event in Melbourne and being paid a hundred and fifty thousand dollars a day. I was going to send all my guys down there, but when I worked out that it was going to cost three thousand dollars a head to go to the event, plus food, accommodation and flights, and them being away the day before and after, it was going to be extremely expensive.

The cost effective alternative was to bring him to our office in Brisbane. I was convinced that I was going to get the money back pretty quickly, off the back of our salespeoples' motivation, the motivation of our trainers, and the involvement of everyone else in the company. To me, it was great value. Easier said than done. Talk about hard to get, Jordan had more security than the US president and his people wouldn't return our calls or respond to our emails.

At the time, I'd just taken Alicia Holker on as my personal assistant and gave her the job of pinning Jordan down. Like everything else she's since done for me, she went at it ferociously. For a month, she hunted him down. Finally, Rachel, his personal assistant, got in touch with Alicia and said that Jordan had agreed to talk to us.

But Alicia's challenge didn't end there. We received a huge list of everything we had to do for Jordan's visit. For example, sushi had to be available, along with freshly baked choc chip cookies, Red Bull Tropical Edition, his favourite Gatorade, special sandwiches, fresh fruit platters, cheese plates, and fresh croissants. The list went on and on.

His driver had to be on call at all times, and the car had to have a reclining back seat for his bad back. A reclining back seat? As it happened there's only one vehicle, a particular Mercedes, that has a reclining back seat. Did they tell us that? No, Alicia had to scour around to find that out.

Orchestrating the details of the entire visit and event, needless to say, Alicia was stressed to the max. The function area of the establishment we were having the event in had to have its green room equipped with everything he required there too.

We were sitting with Jordan the day before the event. The large boardroom table was groaning under the weight of all this food and there were only three of us there. At lunch time, more food arrived. And then during the afternoon, even more. In the meantime, Jordan had eaten virtually nothing.

'What's with all this fucking food?' Jordan asked. 'There's so much of it. What's going on?'

'Well, mate,' I said. 'That's all on the list of stuff we got from your assistant, Rachel.'

'Oh my fucking God,' he said. 'That explains a lot.'

It transpired that Jordan's assistant watches him closely and whenever he takes a bite or nibble of anything she, assuming he likes it, notes it down as a requirement. It turned out that he normally hardly ate at all and didn't like any of the food there. The only thing he really did want was the car with the reclining back seat. That was non-negotiable.

Alicia did such a brilliant job that when Rachel left Jordan, she went off on loan from us to work as Jordan's PA for six months, travelling all over the world, organising his events and everything for him. Although Jordan can be very aggressive with staff and difficult to work for, Alicia was perfect for the job, and he absolutely loved her.

He absolutely loved our company too. He said that we had the best culture, all of our guys were so happy, and it was just a great feeling the minute he walked through the door. The atmosphere told him that we had a successful company. He immediately wanted to be a part of us and to stay on longer.

We discussed a strategy; he would stay an extra day and do some more consulting, and we'd work together to plan a way forward. He ended up staying another week after that, and we'd only paid for two days. He asked Rachel to clear his schedule to do that.

He and I had a lot in common and hit it off together as friends. We had similar personalities. We soon moved forward for him to train our sales guys ethically. Ethics was a key essential factor for both of us, because that's what he was about, and everyone would jump all over him if it wasn't. Of course they would, and we knew people were watching us.

At that point, he brought Leigh in. Leigh would replace Jordan on his two weeks off. He knew Leigh and trusted him. As I've said, Leigh had already had a sales team that he'd built up over the years and he loved everything that our business had going for it. It also gave him an opportunity to work long-term with Jordan.

Boot camps or seminars, if you research Jordan and what he does now, everything about him is about being ethical. In the two events I'd been to, everything was about ethics. I'd studied his sales and his strategy, which is called the 'Straight Line Strategy' and it's ethical. I'd been using his strategy since the boot camp and we were getting fantastic results out of it.

The whole training industry excited the hell out of me. It's a great industry, and it's an industry crying out for ethical reform. Not only that, it's an industry that people need. So, we've got the best product on the planet, people need it, so why wouldn't people take it? Shouldn't it be the easiest sale? It's a funded qualification so people are going to be given recognition for work they've already been doing, plus given new skills.

It sounds like a walk-up sale for anybody, but it just isn't. People struggle to sell it because it sounds too good to be true. One of the first things that Jordan said to me is, 'The most important part about sales is the truth well told.' That was all we needed to tell anyone, we didn't need to tell them anything that wasn't true, we just needed to tell them the truth, but we needed to find a better way of doing it. That's what Jordan is good at. That was the extraordinary talent he brought to the table. Teaching the sales guys a better way of explaining it, but also getting them to listen, so what better person to listen to than the best trainer on the planet? At least you know you're going to get the salespeople in the room and they're actually going to be attentive, and then go out and give it a go.

Jordan could see that other RTOs were making money unethically, and saw that as a big an opportunity for us as I did. Right from the beginning of my career in the training industry, I saw that the biggest opportunity was the lack of professionalism in it. It should be the most professional industry in our country, whereas it appears to be the least. It should be heavily regulated and that's what they'd have you believe, but it's not regulated at all. It's wide open for mistakes and malpractice.

When I see something like that, I don't see an opportunity to rape and pillage, I see an opportunity to build a large, sustainable company for an industry that needs it. It needs people to come in and do the right thing. I can make more money from doing things right than I can from doing things wrong. Jordan saw things the same way.

I explained what this industry was all about to Jordan over the phone and via email before he actually got here. Obviously, I wanted to prep him on everything before he came to talk to and address our whole company. I'd already explained to him what our business was about and, over calls that were sometimes over an hour and half long, Jordan got an in-depth understanding of my belief in ethical practices.

When Jordan first came to the company, he didn't want to walk around and meet all the people, he wanted to really see the business. His priority was to look at every system we had and look at our paperwork. He went right through the whole company. He didn't want to have a conversation, he wanted to see our set-up and what went where.

He wanted to know where the flaws were. When he met Wendy, our compliance officer, the first thing he said was, 'Wendy, now be honest, tell me what it is that we're not doing right. I understand that you've been doing your best, but if I'm going to be here, people are going to look at what we're not doing correctly and we're going to have to fix that. Tell me what we're not doing right so we can fix it.'

Wendy absolutely loved him, because she already had an open cheque book and he was pretty much confirming what I'd told her. He said, 'You've got an open cheque book for compliance because while I've got anything to do with the company, compliance is going to have to be one hundred percent.' We all knew the company was going to get a good, hard look simply because he was on board, but I couldn't see what the problem was because we weren't doing anything wrong.

Jordan asked Wendy where the bodies were buried, and she did come up with one thing. It's a strange one because the government provides all this training money and yet they require the student to pay twenty or thirty dollars in student fees. If they're not paid, the students aren't eligible to get their qualification. It was just a compliance rule, but we weren't following up on it. We'd tell the students about the fees because we were required to do so, but weren't collecting them. Wendy admitted that the issue was something that would concern her in an audit, so we went away and came up with a strategy to get students to pay their fees.

DEALING WITH THE HEAD TRASH

I drive people, and I see that as my main talent. I talk to my guys often and it mightn't be the right conversation, but when things are a little bit tense and the pressure's on, the conversation often goes like this: 'You know what, this company's going forwards and I know I'm going to be here next week. But I'm the only person I know who is going to be here next week.'

Everyone's got their own ways of doing things, and, generally, I'm not really interested in their way. Everyone has good ideas, and you have to listen to them, I get that, but at the end of the day I want what I want and I always get what I want. Every now and then I have to pull people up and remind them. 'It's okay that you've got your ideas and you want to do things your way, but we're not doing it your way, we're doing it my way.'

I'm also a great believer that everybody makes mistakes. One hundred percent, I'm going to make mistakes — we're all going to make mistakes. But, as long as only one of us is making the mistakes, the mistakes are going to be fewer. If we're all making mistakes and doing things our own way we're going to have even more mistakes. The right people take this on board and accept it, and they are the ones I want to stay.

I'm quite a perfectionist and I think anyone who's worked with me will know that. If something's not right, we'll keep doing it until it is right. I like to think that's my secret to success as well — getting it right, and making sure it's good enough.

I had an argument over the weekend with a very good friend of mine. We went to the footy together and he said that if his name doesn't appear in this book he's never going to talk to me again. He said, 'Paint me in a good light, a bad light, I don't care, but my name has to be in there.'

Adrian and I (there you go buddy, you owe me $100,000) go back a bit, and when everything fell over at Face-to-Face and our funding was withdrawn, and people couldn't afford their drug habits, or whatever they had, anymore, I had these two guys come into the office and stand over me. They were representing one of our salespeople who hadn't been paid.

Adrian always tries to stick up for me. I'm not the sort of person who likes that. I don't want anyone sticking up for me, I like to do my own thing, I like to fight my own battles. The last thing I want is for anyone to think that I don't fight my own battles. I've made that very clear to Adrian because he'd done something for me earlier on which I'd asked him not to do. I let him know that he didn't have to look out for me. He's a really nice guy, honest and loyal, and he'd worked for me as a trainer in the transport industry.

So a couple of goons turned up to my office and locked the door behind themselves. Then things got a little uncomfortable. They stood over me, threatened to cut my ears off, threatened to harm my family, and kill me if I didn't write them a cheque for $170,000.

'Guys,' I said. 'I don't have a hundred and seventy thousand dollars. Do whatever you like, I don't have it.' This went on for about forty-five minutes, locked in my office with my life being threatened. To be honest, I was somewhat concerned. They took my phone, they took everything from me, and they threatened me that the guy's brother-in-law was in the Russian mafia.

The deal with our sales staff was that they get paid as we get paid. That way it's retractable. It stops them from going out and enrolling the wrong people into the wrong qualifications. If they do that, they're not going to pass, and then we're not going to get paid.

This happened sometimes. There were sales guys who would do that and expect to get paid, and they just don't get paid in those situations. So this guy had about three thousand dollars that he thought was owed to him and he was chasing me for a hundred and seventy thousand dollars.

In the end I said, 'Look, I've got thirty thousand dollars in the bank, I can draw that out and give it to you but you're not going to get anything else.'

'Do you really want the mafia coming around to your family?' he said.

'Look mate,' I replied. 'You're going to get fuck all sitting here. I have to walk into accounts, I'll get Elena to organise it, give the bank a call to get thirty thousand dollars out.'

'We'll just walk down there,' he said.

'Mate,' I replied. 'You can walk down to the bank and ask for thirty thousand but they're not going to give it to you in cash, you have to call them and arrange it first. So, how about I get a loaner to give them a call and arrange it, I'll get your thirty thousand dollars and we're done.'

Agreeing to that, they escorted me to the accounts office, where I said to Elena, 'Can you call the Westpac bank and ask them to organise thirty thousand dollars?'

'Paul,' she replied. 'We can't do that.'

'Elena,' I said. 'Just do it please.'

So Elena gets on the phone, and then says, 'OK, it'll be ready to pick up at two o'clock this afternoon.'

It was nine o'clock in the morning at that time, so I told the boys, 'OK, we'll pick the money up at two o'clock this afternoon, so I'll see you later.'

'Well mate,' they said. 'What we're going to be doing is going for a drive for the rest of the day until that happens.'

'No offence,' I said. 'But you guys aren't my type. I'm not going to go driving with you for the rest of the day. We're done now, I did what I told you I was going to do.'

'No, you're getting in the car.'

'No I'm not.'

I then shut the door and locked it.

I've done a lot of charity work for different people including the police in the area, so I rang a couple of friends there. They sent someone around to have these guys removed. I also gave my friend Adrian a call, and he came around just to make sure everything was okay.

Some of the guys in his club knew the Russian guys who were going to come around and hurt my family. That evening, not only did those same Russians give the sales guy a call to let him know they wouldn't be doing anything for him, but there was also a car sitting outside his house. He got a call, 'See the car across the road? I hope it doesn't have to come back.' So that's one situation where Adrian helped me out, and he's done a lot of that sort of thing for me when people have tried to get heavy, or tried to stand over me for money. He's a great guy and he's been a great friend.

I'm a very strong believer that you can't measure a man by the amount of weight he can carry in his arms. It's the weight he can carry on his shoulders that you can measure him by.

And, it's not until you hit hard times that people get measured. Out of three hundred and twenty people that we had when things went pear-shaped at Face-to-Face, I can count on one hand the number of people who stayed positive and loyal throughout that time, including my daughter Natasha, and Erin Feeney. I didn't rip anybody off, everybody knows very well that the state government still owes us four point eight million dollars, and they took my money just as they took their money. But, everyone needs someone to blame, or someone to hung out to dry.

One guy unaffected by it all was Adrian. He was there day in and day out and I didn't have any money to pay him — not a cent. He was there because he liked me and he liked what we'd stood for, and what we'd done. He'd had a good time working there and he respected that, and he was just a genuine person. So I did something for him, and that's what we were arguing about at the footy. You thought I'd forgotten, didn't you?

I helped him get started in his own little business. I did a bit of a wheel and deal with another RTO in the transport industry and we put a contract together, a partnership agreement, and got him to start training before he actually had to spend any money on it.

It's actually going really well for him now; he's making good money every month. As I was looking for something else to get into, I had the opportunity to do it with him, but my problem was, with everything that's happened, if I involved myself with his business, there's a good chance it would get shut down. The department of training and education are going to continue their witch-hunt and go after anything I'm involved in.

Adrian won't give up though. He's continuously asked me to be part of his business, and asked me again on the footy weekend. 'Buddy,' I said. 'I can't. It's not that I don't want to help, it's just that I don't want to jeopardise it for you.'

He kept on, 'Paul, don't you see the opportunity that you've given me, and do you not see what you've done for me? Do you not see you've given me a life when I'd not long got out of prison, and I didn't have a lot going on in my life?'

'Mate,' I replied. 'I don't see, and I think it's bullshit, because at the end of the day, it's ten percent actions and ninety percent attitude. Everyone makes their own luck and everyone creates their own attitude.'

I didn't create his attitude, I'm not the one who told him to be a positive person, I'm not the one who made him jump up, dust himself off and want to start again even though he lost money with everything that happened. I didn't do that, he did that. And that was the argument. I'm damned if it was me who made him who he is. People are who they are and that determines how successful they're going to be. It's got nothing to do with the opportunities that come up because those opportunities come up every day. It's just a matter of whether you want to see them or not, and whether you chase after them or not. It all comes down to the attitude of the person. I may have given him a small window of opportunity, but without the right attitude and without the right drive, it means nothing. When you talk about success, it's all about your attitude towards life.

There's a saying, 'Don't let your body language speak louder than your words.' However, most people do let their body language speak louder than their words. Ninety percent, in fact. If someone bites their nails, it makes my blood boil. Chewing gum with their mouths open, chewing food with their mouths open, cracking their finger joints, there's a whole lot of things.

THE TRUTH WELL TOLD

Doing these things opens a window to the soul. For example, a nail-biter is nervy and lacks confidence. They may deny it, but there's a reason why they're biting their nails, there's a reason why they have a nervous twitch. Another is that the hands-on-the-hips person is a little bit full of themselves. All those little tell-tale signs shout out to me. People's body language does speak louder than their words.

Sometimes, that insight is as irritating as hell. My brother Duane irritates me with his body language. He drives me mad just being around him even though he may not say a word. Body language never lies. Not unless you're very good at body language and are able to control it. My wife can't read body language and she'll fall into anything. She'll get annoyed at me for reading somebody and she gets angry at me because she thinks I'm stereotyping people and judging them. Well, maybe I am.

∽

I had a conversation with my daughter last night. She asked me if I was angry about having to start again. I said, 'No, I'm not.' She told me she would be mad if she lost her company. 'You're looking at it all wrong,' I told her. 'You're looking at it like a business owner, and the difference between a business owner and an entrepreneur is that an entrepreneur can start over again.

Give it all away today and start again tomorrow, and don't care. A business owner can't do that because he doesn't know how. He owns a business and he knows how to run it, but he doesn't know how to start again, and again. An entrepreneur doesn't care because he can.'

For me, starting again is not such a big deal, but I guess the head trash that I have at the moment is. I was so angry last week thinking about it, our state government, and for the witch-hunt that came about.

For example, there's an RTO out there doing so much dodgy training. They've stolen all our resources, they used to steal all our marketing material, they steal everything. One of the directors bought himself a three hundred and sixty thousand dollar Mercedes car for cash last week off state funding, and I know these guys are non-compliant and doing the wrong thing. And then they close us down when we were doing the right thing because we supposedly had the wrong person working for us and the media spun it badly on us.

What's making me feel worse is that at the end of the financial year, every year, they release the new VET (Vocational Education and Training) Investment Plan, which details the Queensland Government's seven-hundred-and-fifty-four-million-dollar investment in vocational education and training in the new financial year.

They have all the different qualifications on the plan and how much funding is available for each qualification. It also states the eligibility criteria for the students and the RTOs that will be able to offer that funding. That was released and, guess what, very little has changed.

So, when they said to us, 'Don't feel like you're being singled out, we're going to be doing this across the board,' they haven't done much that I can see. We were absolutely singled out. I have to put all of that out of my mind because the last thing I want to do is be angry, particularly about other companies who are doing well. I should be happy for them. I should only be angry that ours got singled out.

THE WITCH HUNT

We got audited for a month and haven't yet been given an audit report. Can you believe that? They've closed us down, audited us for a month, could find little wrong, and they haven't paid us or given us the report. We've asked DET so many times for our money, we've given them the opportunity to pay us and we've taken them to court. And, by not giving us an audit report, they're clearly shooting themselves in the foot.

On top of that, after they audited me, they audited another RTO, which I've already mentioned, and I know the person who ran the audit in there because she used to do work for us. The first thing the department said was, 'Does this look familiar?' Having spent four weeks with us, the auditors knew our resources very, very well. It was clear that RTO had stolen all of ours.

When they audited us, they then recommended that our registration be terminated because they considered that our resources weren't compliant. Be mindful that that audit wasn't against resources, that audit was against the funding and the dates and the eligibility criteria, and those sorts of things. It's ASQA that's supposed to audit against resources. But they recommended to ASQA that our resources were non-compliant and ASQA closed our three RTOs.

ASQA emailed to let me know that they were giving twenty-one days' notice, that they were going to terminate our registration for all three RTOs off the back of the allegations made by DET, and if we wanted to dispute that decision we had to let them know. I emailed them back and told them that I did dispute their decision, saying the decision didn't make any sense.

We had no money, and DET had held our money back, so we'd have to respect whatever decision they made. They closed the RTOs twenty-one days later. They didn't come and audit us beforehand, they closed us down without even coming to investigate whether the allegations were true. Even worse, DET audited an RTO straight after us, knew that they had all our resources, and didn't close them down, and I'm unaware of any recommendations that their resources were non-compliant. But the story is bigger than that, so let's back up a bit.

A bit further back, we received an audit notification from the Department of Education and Training to audit our systems. The audits would usually occur once every one to two years. It wasn't our first DET audit for Face-to-Face training but it was the first since we had grown. We were excited about it because we knew we were doing our best. Our business had grown and the audit would give validation to our own thoughts of striving to be way above standard. It would give us an opportunity to showcase what we had going on. Off the back of that, we would be able to grow again. Also, at that point, we were paying an external industry auditor to come in two days a month to make sure we were compliant. It was costing us eight thousand dollars a month, but we wanted to make sure we were doing the right thing. We were very confident and very enthusiastic.

The DET auditors give you a list of students and five days to get together the complete files for them to look at. I think the list was for about seventy-five students of Face-to-Face Training. The three-day audit blew out to five days. There were five auditors and they had to go through the seventy-five files and make sure the systems were right and the training was right. That audit went quite well.

In the training industry there is something called continuous improvement and everyone has to abide by it. We have to have a continuous improvement register to ensure we are looking for ways to improve. So of course the auditors are going to find both improvement and also some small non-compliances. The biggest part of the audit is the good faith clause. Everyone makes mistakes but, as long as you are acting in good faith and not trying to rip anyone off, or taking the government's money and not providing the training, then everything else can be fixed.

We passed the good faith clause with flying colours. They did find some minor non-compliances but that was always going to happen. I have never heard of anyone in this industry be audited without a few small non-compliances. That was discussed at the exit meeting with the DET auditors and they made some recommendations back to their boss. It all went well and we were really happy with it.

It was about a month after that that we received notification for another audit on another RTO of mine (there are three altogether). They were the same auditors as the last time. The audit went pretty much the same as the first and, at the end of it we asked them to do a DET health check. This comes with amnesty. The auditors come to the office and look at everything in the business including processes, and they will tell you if you are on the right track, and doing the right thing or not. We wanted that. We wanted to make sure we were compliant with everything. They booked us in for three days later.

The day before the DET auditors were due, we received a phone call from them saying their boss had cancelled the DET check. We were really annoyed and disappointed because a DET check is a standard process within the industry. I sent an email to Linda Bradley, the director of DET, asking for a meeting. We wanted to know what the problem was. She agreed to meet with me, but the very afternoon before the meeting was due she emailed and cancelled it. We then organised another DET check from another department but again someone upstairs cancelled that.

We didn't realise that because we had grown so fast, we were taking a lot of work from others in the industry and a tsunami of envy had developed. RTOs, trainers and sales guys were ringing DET complaining about us. They were saying we were providing dodgy training and doing the wrong thing. It was simply sour grapes but they were complaints nonetheless. We knew about some of it happening because we were getting questions from DET and ASQA.

In the background, something else was festering. Donna Hedley, one of our sales team, was making a lot of trouble. She was arguing with and abusing other salespeople, and we had to have a couple of talks with her about it. She was becoming quite vindictive and not being a team player at all.

There were two other people like that; Doug Baumber and Ryan, his nephew. They were also causing a lot of trouble within the team. They were openly telling people they had seen Jordan and myself walking out of the office with bloody noses because we were snorting so much coke. They were spreading rumours that we were both sleeping with my assistant, Alicia, and sleeping with other girls in the company. They were also talking about how dodgy we were in forcing them into using high-pressured sales tactics.

All that couldn't be further than the truth. The one thing that we used to train is 'the truth well told' and we didn't want to train any other way. We even taped every one of our training sessions, in case anyone disputed our methodology.

We let Doug and Ryan go. We knew they were moonlighting with another RTO, so they weren't working for us one hundred percent. Instead, they were taking our secrets into another RTO. We did do it in the nicest possible way.

About a week after that, the compliance team brought in a pile of enrolments that happened in Townsville the day before. Donna Hedley wanted to be paid for them but we knew she hadn't been in Townsville that day. She had been in Brisbane. Enrolments are a legal document, a contract between the student and us, and these had the students' signatures on them. There was no way that they were the students' signatures. Part of an enrolment is that the student provides a copy of their licence. Donna had the copies the students had emailed to her. So we knew that she forged the signatures on the enrolment forms.

We had good cause to sack her right there, but we gave her an opportunity to be retrained. She wasn't up for that at all, told us where to go, and quit.

People that have common enemies come together, and that's what Donna Hedley and Doug and Ryan Baumber did. They went to the media. Not just to *60 Minutes* but to every media entity they could. At this point, only Channel 7 knew that Jordan was with us.

The gang of three told the media that Jordan Belfort was working in Brisbane, was sleeping with staff, and pushing high-pressure sales. They also said that there was absolutely no training after the sale, and that the salesmen and trainers didn't get paid. All that had huge implications. Add to it that we were taking taxpayers money for doing nothing and not paying anybody except Jordan Belfort, the media would smell blood in the water.

The gang made their claims to *A Current Affair*, *60 Minutes*, the ABC — anyone they possibly could. Doug and his nephew were also sending messages to the sales guys to say that Face-to-Face was not going to be operating any longer because they were going to have us closed down. He was doing that because he'd made a deal with another RTO and wanted the sales guys to come and work for him. He would get a commission for bringing the sales guys over. And, in the end, he did get his own way.

At the time, we had no idea this was happening. Out of the blue we had the media following our sales guys around. Every morning we would have sales and training meetings where the media would come through the office and then follow the sales guys onto sites. They'd ask leading questions like, 'Why are you signing people up just so you can't train them?' or 'Don't you realise you're working for a company that's ripping people off?'

Not only were they talking to our students, sales guys and trainers on site but they were also making phone calls to DET and ASQA, asking them the same leading questions. Eventually it was on TV. They were also asking the minister for training, Yvette D'Ath, who had also been the attorney general, the same leading questions and had it all on tape. Unbeknown to us, this was the real reason DET kept cancelling their meetings with us. They were circling their wagons rather than deal with us. Here we were trying to touch base with someone, trying to work out what was going on because we weren't doing anything wrong, and nobody wanted to talk to us. We were starting to feel a bit victimised.

At this point, we contracted a PR company to come in and help look after what was going on. The company dealt with the media and knew all the media people. We also hired a lawyer to take out an injunction against the false claims from Donna Hedley and Doug and Ryan Baumber. It cost us eighty thousand dollars for the injunction to stop the information that they were using to try to destroy our company via the media.

Our PR lady contacted *60 Minutes* by phone, but they denied even knowing who we were. They denied having even spoken to anyone from the company. On the same day as those phone calls, they would be going out on site questioning our people. We were offering *60 Minutes* statements at the time because we wanted them to know the truth. If they wanted to ask about high-pressure sales, we were offering them our training tapes. We offered them all our tapes so they could see the facts, with the only stipulation being that they must play the whole piece, not do a hatchet job by editing them. If they wanted the truth, the truth was there to tell. Needless to say, they did not want the tapes.

We also offered an interview. Everyone knows what *60 Minutes* did to Jordan previously, so he said, 'Tell them to get fucked, I'll never give them anything'. I told Jordan that that wouldn't help our cause, so he finally agreed to talk to them. We wanted *60 Minutes* to tell us what it was they wanted to talk about prior to the interview and we would give them as much time as they wanted. Again they didn't go with that.

Late on the Friday afternoon before the weekend they aired the *60 Minutes* programme, they asked us for a statement. It was all too late and they were very aware of that. That gave them the right to say on their show that they asked for a statement but we didn't give them one. There were so many horrible media tactics that went into that dodgy story.

On top of the injunction against Donna Hedley and the Baumbers, we received a letter from the *60 Minutes* solicitors saying they understood and were taking the injunction very seriously. They would not use anything for their story from Hedley and the Baumbers. Then they aired the *60 Minutes* programme on Sunday night with Donna Hedley and they used everything. The most we could have sued them for was three hundred thousand and the lawyers would have cost more than that to do anything about it. But, the damage was done and we didn't take any further action.

The biggest part of their one hundred percent hatchet job was a guy with an excavator. We knew that was going to happen. The media had actually contacted a company that we do plant training for and asked them if they would be involved. *60 Minutes* told them what they wanted to do and the plant company gave us the heads up and then declined.

Obviously, the media went to another company and used them instead. What *60 Minutes* wanted to do was bring someone on site and demonstrate that we had given him an excavator competency and that he wasn't competent in using an excavator at all.

The guy that they took out on site had been given an excavator competency by us. He owned a three-tonne excavator and a landscaping company. All the guy wanted was a competency for his three-tonner. That was what the competency rating was for. When *60 Minutes* took him out on site, on camera, they didn't ask him if he had ever operated an excavator, they asked him if he had ever operated a thirty-tonne excavator (like the one that they had him sitting in on site). They said to him, 'Do you think an excavator of this size could kill someone if you didn't know what you were doing?' and the guy said, 'Yes, of course it could. I could easily kill someone. I wouldn't even know how to start this or where the brake is.'

Of course he didn't, and nor did he want to. He never had any intention of operating a thirty-tonne excavator, he just wanted to have a competency rating for his three-tonner.

And that was their story. Crime: we had given him an excavator competency when he didn't know how to drive a thirty-tonne excavator. That would have been a fair story except that there is no size limit on the type of excavator you can use when you have an excavator competency certificate. We don't make those rules up. They are the federal government's rules.

The first thing I did on the Monday morning when I went into work was pull the guy's file. We had photos of him in his excavator because we take photos of everything. We always required photographic proof from the trainers. It was all right then, I knew the trainer and realised that he was one of the most effective, conscientious and skilled trainers we had.

With a light heart, I addressed the sales team, the trainers, and everyone else in the company. 'Guys,' I said. 'We've been in defence mode for the last six weeks with the media, and was that all they had?'

If that was the best they could do, I was worried about nothing. I also sent an email to Linda Bradley, director of DET and to ASQA explaining how the *60 Minutes* report was a hatchet job. As usual, I got nothing in return from either of them and gave it no more thought.

About a week later, we got an email and a letter on the same day from DET. I had repurchased a ten percent share of the company from Wade Grundon, one of our sales trainers, and also one from my cousin, Rob Ford. You can't just change control of a company, a director or a shareholder, until you ask permission from DET. All that was happening but it takes four months. Suddenly, on the same day, I had permission for the changes I wanted. So I'm thinking, everything's good, they are happy with me and the company, so I made the changes.

A couple of days after that I got a breach of contract notification for all of my state government funding contracts. They said I had changed control without permission. But, when I got permission, I did have the right to change the director on ASIC (Australian Securities and Investments Commission). After doing so, I had to send them the new ASIC report to say I'm the new director. I had a compliance team of thirty-five people and was very strict about doing anything wrong. After all, we had to guard the goose that laid the golden egg.

What I didn't realise was that I had been set up. I told DET that I had been given permission to make the changes, but DET then told me that it was conditional permission. I had to send them the ASIC notification before I could make the changes. I couldn't get ASIC notification until I made the changes. It was DET's rules and I stuck to them. The rules were a little bit ambiguous and you could read them either way. DET's solicitors agreed that I was probably right. However, they said that verbally but they wouldn't put it into writing.

Two days after overcoming that breach, at ten to five on a Friday afternoon, three letters were hand delivered to us. They were notices to terminate our funding contract without cause. Clause 21 of our funding contracts states that the department can terminate the contract without a reason, but the department has to give twenty-one days' notice to do so. Clearly, we were being set up another way.

We immediately went into clearing the decks mode. Our state contract was still on for the next twenty-one days, so the very next day I let the sales guys know that we weren't taking any more students. We would service all the students we had for the next twenty-one days as best we could, and we would finish off any students that could be finished off.

We brought in three different RTOs and did a deal with them. They were happy to take on any students we couldn't finish off and they were happy to pay the sales guys for the enrolments. We did not ask the sales guys to repay what we had paid them for the students up front. We also introduced the sales guys to many other RTOs in the industry. I kept my trainers on for the next twenty-one days but moved the sales guys on. I just wanted everyone to get out with the minimal amount of harm.

THAT EVIL AUDIT

As we focused all our energy on chasing up the money that the government was withholding, we received an audit notification. There would be eight auditors starting in a week's time, and they didn't know how long the audit would take. Strangely, they didn't give us the names of students they wanted to look at this time, so this was all a bit new to us.

New too was the eight auditors' attitudes when they arrived. They were stand-offish and, from the start, appeared to be on a mission to nail us whatever it took. One of them only wanted to check that we'd collected the required student fees. *60 Minutes* had stated that we hadn't and we proved that to be bullshit. The other auditors were going to examine the quality of our training and the eligibility of our students.

What we didn't realise and found out later was that of the eight auditors there, four of the supposed auditors were not actually trained auditors, this amounted to nothing more than fraud by misrepresentation on the part of DET. They worked for a firm that dealt with liquidation. They didn't make us aware of that at the time. The government had actually outsourced to the liquidation firm and brought them in to use them as auditors.

Those guys had no training whatsoever in auditing quality of training, and all they were there for was to look at eligibility criteria. They were looking at copies of Medicare cards or copies of licences that we had to have for student identification. What they were looking for were blurry copies so they could say that those students were ineligible to be enrolled because the auditor couldn't read the copy. They were trying to pull us up on anything so that the money owed us wouldn't have to be paid. This went on for four weeks. The government owed us close to five million dollars and obviously didn't intend to pay any of it.

At the time, I was fuming at the direction they'd taken, but also very confident. We knew we hadn't done anything wrong and embraced the audit because we knew they would find little out of place and we'd end up getting paid. We were among the top five percent in the industry for compliance because we had spent so much time and money on getting it right. I knew they wanted to close us down and accepted that. All I wanted was to clear the decks and move on.

As it continued, the audit became more and more aggressive. At first the auditors wanted to look at fifty files, then one hundred files, and then more. When the audit started, I asked the lead auditor how long he thought it would take.

He said, 'Normally three days but, sometimes, up to five'. At this stage we were no longer doing any training and had no income, but I still had to pay my staff to be there to give the auditors whatever they wanted. The last thing we wanted was to give DET a reason not to pay us. It was an expensive exercise.

After five days, they informed us that they'd see us the next week because they weren't done. They inferred that we were lying, asked to see more and more files, and still couldn't find what they were looking for. They clearly thought it would be a walk in the park, they'd rip us to pieces and claw back the four point eight million dollars owed to us. It didn't happen for them and not at any stage did they soften up. They just asked to see more and more.

In those first weeks, they were rummaging through the files, leaving paperwork all over the desks, and totally messing up our filing system. Then, when they'd been given a hundred files, they would come back to us and claim twenty files had things missing from them, like the copies of the Medicare cards or birth certificates. Our girls would have a look in the files and would find at least ninety-five percent of the items that the auditors were claiming were missing. Flicking through, the auditors had simply missed them. Then, when we produced the missing items, the auditors accused us of getting on the phone to the students and getting copies of the licenses or Medicare cards and placing them in the files.

The lead auditor actually admitted that he was frustrated and insisted that if a file had anything missing from it, it was not to be removed from the room. We had to examine the paperwork right there. I assigned two full-time girls to go through the files the auditors believed were incomplete. Sometimes hard copy information missing from a file would have been scanned onto our system, but we did have it.

After the second week the auditors were even more frustrated. They weren't allowing files to be taken out of the room, but we were still finding the information for them. They were convinced we were cheating somehow. Then they gave us just one hour a day to find information they claimed was missing from files. After checking two hundred files, they might give us thirty to look through in only one hour. The pressure on everyone was appalling.

We were giving them anything they wanted. At first they asked for names, and then they were asking for a hundred files and that's what we gave them. Then they were asking for ten or twenty boxes of files. Not finding what they expected, they decided to go through every file with a fine-toothed comb.

The auditors were making such a mess of our files. They were claiming missing paperwork and we would find it on the desk where the auditor had been. The integrity of our files was being compromised and we could see the writing on the wall. If they were to lose a piece of paper out of a file because of the untidy way they were doing the audit, we were going to have pay that qualification back — from a mistake they had made.

I had to do something so, after the second week, I had eight cameras put in the room. It was a very large room — part of the call centre. I then projected the camera feed onto a screen so they could see everything we could. Everyone was on the same page now and the auditors knew that we had it on camera.

I had also put a guy on a desk full time, and the auditors had to sign every file in and out. I then knew which auditor had which file and at what time. If anything was missing from the file I could then go back and look at what was on camera from the time the file had been signed out. One day they put a file down and later they claimed that I had come and taken it. We went back and had a look at what was on camera and it showed that one of the auditors had taken the file and put it somewhere else.

The auditors spent all day compiling the twenty or thirty files that supposedly had something missing and we were given only the one hour for all those files to be ratified. But, the girls loved it and thrived on it. They called it the 'hour of power', and every afternoon between four and five, for the next two weeks, five or six girls would tear into the suspect files. Then, when they found the 'missing' paperwork, they'd high-five in front of the auditors and say, 'There you go, there's another one for you.' The auditors were becoming short-tempered and very despondent.

I still believe that the auditors weren't lying about the 'missing' items. I think they were simply incompetent. And we proved them wrong day in and day out. Fifty percent of them weren't DET employees. I estimate that DET had spent around four hundred thousand dollars on a legal team trying to do something they didn't know anything about, on top of paying their own guys.

Towards the end of four weeks, John, our CFO, asked the lead auditor what was going on, and how long was it going to take. We had never gone through an audit before that had gone over five days, and those guys had been there for almost a month. We all felt very confident when we arrived in the mornings but by the afternoons morale was shot. We were tired of being the object of an obvious witch-hunt.

The auditors were clearly exhausted too. Whenever they phoned their boss and found out they had to come back the next day their demeanour changed and their depression was obvious. They'd had enough. By the end I think the auditors felt sorry for us as well. I believe they were reporting directly to Linda Bradley, the director of DET. It went to the very top.

One of the auditors mentioned that they had to reach a particular number so they didn't have to pay us any money. And that's what it was all about. DET still haven't paid any money, nor have they given us an audit report. We still don't know how many infractions counted against us in financial terms, but I sincerely believe it was very few.

Throughout the audit, they would find silly things. In DET's eligibility guidelines, it said that a student had to have a current driver's licence and a Medicare card. It doesn't say current Medicare card. A lot of people use expired Medicare cards and they are still accepted by doctors. Any time they found a copy of an expired card we would have to pay back the full amount of money paid to us for that student. I argued the point with them at the time, saying that the guidelines didn't state current Medicare card, and they would say, 'Well that is what the guideline means.' If they were going to do it to us, they should have done it to the whole industry. Interestingly, DET has since changed the guidelines.

There is a site on the Internet called 'DET Connect'. A trainer is required to get onto DET Connect to make sure their students are eligible. If the student already holds all of the units in Certificate III qualification, that student is not eligible. However, there was a problem with how some RTOs loaded information onto the system. When a student had done one unit and the wrong button was pressed, it would show that the student had achieved the full qualification.

For example, if a student had done a working at heights course it was one unit of competency out of a plumbing qualification. If the information is loaded incorrectly, it will probably show that the student has a certificate in plumbing. But, clicking onto that and scrolling down shows only the one unit of competency in the plumbing certificate, not the whole qualification.

DET will tell you that you can't use DET Connect as evidence. It's only a guide. We have an enrolment form where a student asserts that he has never completed a Cert III, yet on DET Connect it shows that he has. That means the student is theoretically ineligible for the funding. The auditors found a heap of students under those circumstances and, although we wanted to show them the anomaly on the DET Connect site, they didn't want to know that. They didn't care. We then phoned some of the students and proved to the auditors that they were eligible. They didn't entertain any of that either. They said they were going to class it as a payback for now and work it out later. But they never did.

So all these things could be argued in a court of law and that's why I believe an audit report hasn't been issued. There was simply not a lot to report on. By law, DET is obliged to give us an audit report. There is a time frame, which is way past due. Instead, they've palmed everything off to their solicitors.

In the lead up to Christmas 2015, I asked for them to pay something to us. I was pleading with them. First fifty percent, then forty, then down to ten percent, so we could at least pay our people's wages. We had to let so many people go unpaid close to Christmas. We could pay people something, but I had people coming around to my house, and I was receiving daily death threats.

DET then asked us a heap of information on our net position. They asked us how much money we had in the bank, how much we owed and what assets we had. So instead of entertaining the idea of paying us the money, they asked us for our complete position so they could look at what they needed to release. Because I wanted to work with them, we were silly enough to give them all the information they wanted. I just wanted our guys paid.

We didn't get paid a cent. It was just a fishing expedition. We were now in an even more vulnerable state because they knew exactly whether or not we had the money to fight them in court.

I had no choice but to start court proceedings a few weeks before Christmas, a judgment against DET so we could pay our bills. It cost around eighty thousand dollars in legal fees and about two weeks to get that underway. The amount of paperwork was incredible — almost twenty thousand pages, because every cent owed has to be itemised.

The state government then had twenty-eight days to reply. That is, to either pay the money, or put up a defence. After thirty-one days, DET still hadn't filed a defence and we still didn't have an audit report. Instead, DET's solicitor sent our solicitor a letter requesting us not to take any legal action without first giving them seven days' notice.

It was legal stalling; we didn't have to accept what they were requesting but if we didn't respond it would be the same as accepting the request. And then the court would frown on it if we took legal action without the seven days' notice.

About two weeks after that, DET, with a small handful of paperwork, issued a counterclaim for six million dollars. They were actually saying forget about the five million DET owed us, they were claiming six million was owed to them; but with nothing to justify it. That was simply another stalling tactic. And, knowing our precarious financial position so well, they also applied to the court for securities of costs.

DET knew very well that we didn't have any money left because they had already done a fishing expedition into our books. They took out securities of costs for five hundred thousand which then tipped us upside down. The court case couldn't move forward until we put that money we didn't have into the federal court account for security. That was just another tactic to stall the case and, to this day, the case hasn't moved forward.

It seems that rather than DET paying their debt to us so we could pay our people, they were prepared to spend to fight us. To this day, it's clearly because Jordan was involved. Fair enough, if they had a bit of egg on their face and had to shut us down through sheer embarrassment, but they went after everyday people who'd done legitimate, honest, hard work and, by hook or by crook, made sure those people wouldn't get paid.

THE STATE OF PLAY

So there you have it — the brutal truth, about me, my work, my people, what I think, and how I think it. You know the real story behind Jordan and how, at my invitation, that crooked, mean old coke-snorting wolf came to ravish the state's funds.

You've also learnt a little something about the training industry. I'll say it again — it's the best industry on the planet, but not the way it's run right now. Let's clean it up guys!

Ready to toss me on the dump? It's up to you. Personally, I don't care if you do. I'll get up, brush myself off, and get right back to it. The difference is — now you know I will.

Oh, and by the way, wouldn't we all love to see that audit report? Really.

ACKNOWLEDGEMENTS

I wish to express my sincere gratitude to the many people who saw me through the writing of this book. To those who provided assistance through their reading, feedback, design, editing and proofreading. I would like to extend that thanks to all of those who have provided me with the life experiences, both positive and negative, that I have drawn upon as subject matter.

This book is dedicated to **Terry Campbell**, a greatly supportive and positive man, who we tragically lost earlier this year. Also, to **Jim Jameson**, who suffers an occupation-related terminal illness and whom I will always be extremely proud to call my father-in-law.

Further, I would like to take this opportunity to dedicate this book to all the people who lost their lives or were injured in accidents which could have so easily been avoided in the construction industry.

All accidents are preventable, and it is only with education, training and ongoing commitment to continuous improvement in the area of health and safety can we make this a reality for all in the future, so that no deaths or accidents will have been in vain.

Paul Conquest

Paul Conquest is a serial entrepreneur. He has launched numerous million-dollar companies from scratch, and has turned the knowledge and experience he has learned along the way into writing this book. He lives by his own practical rules, turning problems into solutions and opportunities to achieve success. The Truth Well Told is his first book. Paul lives in Brisbane, Australia with his wife and six children. If you would like to contact him directly, he is available at paul@qualified.net.au.

www.ingramcontent.com/pod-product-compliance
Lightning Source LLC
Chambersburg PA
CBHW062103080426
42734CB00012B/2735